The Write Beginning

Instruction that starts with the end in mind and guides
students to become more effective writers

L I S A   D O N O H U E

Pembroke Publishers Limited

The Write Beginning is dedicated to my Mom, who, when the doctors told her to go home and *die*, went home to *live*! Time is the gift of immeasurable value.

© **2009 Pembroke Publishers**
538 Hood Road
Markham, Ontario, Canada L3R 3K9
www.pembrokepublishers.com

Distributed in the U.S. by Stenhouse Publishers
480 Congress Street
Portland, ME 04101
www.stenhouse.com

We acknowledge the financial support of the Government of Canada through the Book Publishing Industry Development Program (BPIDP) for our publishing activities.

We acknowledge the assistance of the Government of Ontario through the Ontario Media Development Corporation's Ontario Book Initiative.

Library and Archives Canada Cataloguing in Publication

Donohue, Lisa
   The write beginning : instruction that starts with the end in mind and guides students to become more effective writers / Lisa Donohue.

Includes index.
ISBN 978-1-55138-246-3

   1. English language—Composition and exercises—Study and teaching (Elementary).
I. Title.

LB1576.D634 2009   372.62'3   C2009-903874-9

Editor: Kat Mototsune
Cover Design: John Zehethofer
Typesetting: Jay Tee Graphics Ltd.

Printed and bound in Canada
9 8 7 6 5 4 3 2

FSC
Mixed Sources
Product group from well-managed forests and other controlled sources
Cert no. SW-COC-002358
www.fsc.org
© 1996 Forest Stewardship Council

Contents

Introduction: The End

Why would a book entitled *The Write Beginning* begin with "The End"? It's because the end is the best place to start. Having a clear picture of what a final product will look like ensures that we can identify the important elements and understand how they all fit together purposefully.

Returning from a local big-box store, a young family gathered together to cut open the cardboard box that contained a recently purchased large item of furniture. The box itself seemed rather compact, not at all large enough to contain the bulky item that had been purchased. They anxiously opened the box and began to pull random pieces of wood, bits of iron, and fasteners from it. The pieces quickly spread around the room and in no way resembled the item of furniture that they were hoping to have in the end. Searching through the box, they located the instructions for assembly. Beginning with the largest pieces, they started to combine the elements together in the way that was described in the manual. It was not long before they discovered that they were in over their heads with their construction project, and the frustration level started to escalate. How does one attach a hinge to a door? Do the doors open in or out? Which one goes on the left and which one on the right? How do all the pieces fit together in a way that is meaningful? It was the seven-year-old future engineer who came to the rescue. She eagerly found the lost piece of cardboard that clearly illustrated the final product—the picture on the box. She simply stated: "I know where this piece goes—it shows you on the picture on the box." The family found they could examine the picture of their goal and determine how the pieces should fit together. It wasn't long before the random pieces started to resemble the final product, their goal. Although they needed to carefully follow the step-by-step directions, it was the illustration that kept them focused on the final product. It was their beacon, their target, their exemplar. They were able to measure their progress in terms of how closely their work resembled the target. They knew that, in the end, all the pieces would fit together, and they would have a final product similar to the one on the cover of the box.

This story illustrates the importance of setting clear goals with young writers. If they have a clear picture of the final product, they will find it easier to determine how the seemingly random pieces may fit together. By keeping this target in mind, they will gain the perspective to step back from the frustration of the moment and see the bigger picture. It gives them a clear goal, and they can measure their success as writers in terms of this goal. They understand how and why the pieces fit together, and will find it easier to apply their learning. If writers begin with a clear vision of the final product, the individual skills associated with it seem to lose their randomness and become integral components of the complete piece. Begin with the big picture, break it into the smaller components, then use these components to construct the complete piece. Simple—just like assembling furniture!

We have all heard the adage, "Begin with the end in mind." This is a familiar concept to many in the business world. Stephen Covey's *Seven Habits of Highly Effective People* describes the importance of having a clear vision of a goal and setting a personal mission statement to help reach this desired outcome. This is intended to help align one's actions with values and principles as a way of striving to achieve the desired outcome.

Stephen Covey may have coined the phrase, but the principle is an underlying belief in most successful teaching philosophies. Students need to have a clear vision of the expectations and learning outcomes, as well as the ways in which they will demonstrate their learning. They need a clear vision of the assessment process that will be used to evaluate their work, and they need to see their learning as purposeful, valuable, and authentic. As young writers, they need to understand the final target, identify the components that make it successful, and receive feedback along the way. Rick Stiggins (2006) believes that "students can hit any target that they know about and holds still for them." When we work with students to set clear targets, they are much more able to reach these goals.

What is the End? The end is the final target that we set with our students. It is the final product, the goal that the students need to reach. To begin with the end in mind means that the students have a clear understanding of the product they will be required to produce, knowledge of the elements they need to include, and a thorough understanding of the process with which they will be assessed. This ensures that students are active participants, rather than passive observers, in the assessment process. With assessment-based learning, there is no surprise for students, there is no mystery, and there is an open dialogue between student and teacher. Students have a clear understanding of the target, a realistic understanding of how far they are from it, and what they need to do in order to reach it. When we use assessment-based learning, we are involving our students in understanding the criteria for success and actively participating in creating the tools with which they will be evaluated.

Anne Davies (annedavies.com) describes the role of assessment-based learning: "In order to support student learning, classroom assessment needs to involve students deeply in the assessment process, provide specific, descriptive feedback during the learning, and include evaluative feedback as required to communicate and report progress over time." She states,

> Students need to know what they already know, what needs to be learned and
> what success looks like. Students also need to learn how to guide their own
> learning through being involved in setting and using criteria, giving themselves
> feedback for learning, setting goals, collecting evidence and communicating that
> evidence of learning to others.

As we involve students in their assessment, they become self-reflective self-monitoring learners who assume more responsibility for their learning. They show greater engagement and a deeper understanding of their strengths and needs as learners. When students actively participate in setting goals, they are able to articulate their learning and use assessment as a tool from which they can continue to learn, rather than a final summative evaluation.

Using assessment-based learning to strengthen students' writing is highly beneficial. Not only do young learners become better writers, but they become more competent at articulating their strengths and setting goals for their next piece of work. Using exemplars and mentor texts helps students understand high levels of writing and determine the features of each piece that make it successful. Involving students in setting success criteria enables them to see the elements in each mentor text and set realistic targets to include in their own writing. In this way, we move away from a focus on conventions and toward a focus on content, style, voice, and form. Students need to be encouraged to take risks and try creative things with their writing, improving their word choice and ideas. Involving students in discussions about their writing through descriptive feedback enables young writers to articulate their strengths, needs, and desires for their work. They are able to point out the features they think are strong, experiment with new strategies, and set goals for their continued growth.

CHAPTER 1 *Working with the End in Sight*

The Assessment-Based Writing Process

For years, the writing process has been defined in five recognizable steps: Prewriting, Drafting, Revising, Editing, and Publishing. We recognize that students need to spend time thinking about what they need to write before they write it; they need to take the time to create a draft; they need to revise and edit as a way of improving the piece and preparing it for sharing with others in the final stage.

The Traditional Writing Process
Prewriting
Drafting
Revising
Editing
Publishing

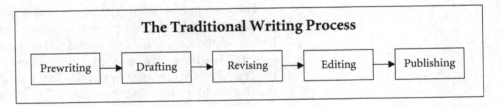

The Traditional Writing Process

Prewriting → Drafting → Revising → Editing → Publishing

The Assessment-Based Writing Process
Prewriting: Establishing Success Criteria
Drafting: The Writing Process
Revising and Editing: Using Descriptive Feedback
Publishing: Sharing, Reflection, and Assessment

However, critically missing from this traditional writing process is the initial goal-setting that students need to do to determine their personal targets for the piece, and the feedback and guidance of the teacher (and self and peers) to gently shape the piece. The writing process is not a linear one as presented in this typical model, where a piece starts at the beginning with students prewriting their ideas, and ends when the piece is published. Instead, the writing process is recursive. This means that the writer is constantly revisiting the previous stages and finding new ways of refining a piece of writing in order to improve it. Writers do not wait until they have completed their first draft to begin revising —they are constantly rereading and reworking the piece, gradually shaping it in the direction that is pleasing to them as authors, while continuing to draft more. Likewise, an author may choose to add to or delete portions of the text that were initially included during the prewriting stage. The writing process is not linear. Instead it is a fluid process: writers understand and set goals for their work; then begin to draft, revise, draft some more; possibly revise again, even revisiting the initial prewriting and adjusting it accordingly; then draft and revise once more in order to bring the piece closer to their goals.

In most writing processes, teacher feedback is given after students have completed the entire writing process and have published a finished piece. Feedback at this point may serve to evaluate or motivate the students' future writing endeavors; however, it does not provide much practical guidance for the task at hand. For this reason, teacher feedback should occur throughout the entire writing process, but is most effective when the student is working on revising the piece. This is when the teacher and student together can reflect on the goals for the piece, measure its success, and refine any areas that need work.

The recursive assessment-based writing process is one that we need to develop in young writers. It is not a simple linear five-step process; instead it is a series of important processes in developing and refining a piece of writing.

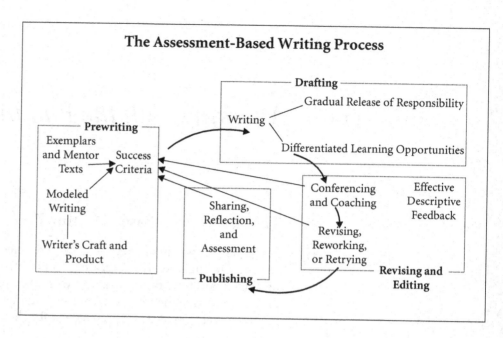

The Assessment-Based Writing Process

The assessment-based writing process is based on the primary belief that all students can achieve their goals, as long as the goals are clear and students have had the opportunity to understand the expectations included in the target. An essential teaching component is the conferencing and coaching stage, at which the teacher provides descriptive feedback to the students. Through this stage, the teacher helps to refine the students' work and bring it closer to their goal.

Prewriting: Establishing Success Criteria

The assessment-based writing process begins with the students developing a clear understanding of the writing goal through the use of mentor texts, exemplars, or modeled writing. The purpose of the prewriting stage is that students develop a key understanding of the piece of writing they will need to create. Through this stage, students will develop a solid understanding of the craft of constructing the writing, the product that they will create, and the features that will make it successful.

Through the examination of mentor texts, exemplars, or modeled writing, students and teacher are able to construct a list of features that make the work successful—the success criteria. This becomes the backbone for their work. The success criteria are the targets that students set for their own writing, and that will serve as the measures of their success. Success criteria can include targets relating to the form of the writing, the ideas included in the writing, the way the writing is communicated, and the way the students use their writing to connect to themselves. They are the key features of a successful piece of writing that students will strive to include in their own work.

For example, when writing a report, students may include the following as success criteria for a piece:

Once students have a clear understanding of the task that is expected of them they will have a much greater chance of meeting with success.

- I will remember to include an introduction and a conclusion that summarizes my main point.
- I will include interesting content and sufficient supporting details.
- I will use conventional spelling, grammar, and punctuation.

- I will evaluate which information is important, and determine if it is suitable to include in the writing. If it is not suitable, I will gather more information.

Before students are asked to write a piece in a particular form, they need to develop their background knowledge about it. They need to have some exposure to the components and purpose associated with the form of writing. Imagine being asked to write a doctoral dissertation, never having seen one before in your life. You probably would struggle with many things; for example, what voice is appropriate, when and how to cite references, and if it is appropriate to include your own opinion on the subject. Many of our students feel the same about being asked to write many forms of writing. For example, some might have very limited experiences with letters; however, we might mistakenly assume that it is a form that they are familiar with. Others may have read many narratives, but never really stopped to think about the elements they contain. Through exposure to exemplars or mentor texts, students are able to develop an understanding of the specific form of writing and attend to the details that are necessary to include in their own work.

As students explore mentor texts and exemplars, we need to help them become conscious of the different parts, as well as the components of writing that make them successful. When sharing mentor texts or exemplars with students, we need to specifically draw their attention to things like how these pieces are constructed and the effect they have on the reader. We can not assume that students will incidentally discover the things we wish them to learn. We need to scaffold their learning by providing a framework for their thinking.

Modeled writing gives the students a clear understanding of the process and product associated with the writing task. When students observe the teacher working through the craft of drafting a piece of work, they are able to develop an understanding of the strategies they will have to apply themselves in order to complete the task. Through modeled writing, the teacher also demonstrates the product that students will work toward. In this way, youngsters are able to develop an understanding of the necessary elements contained in the writing piece. When teachers model writing, they point out when they are thinking of the elements of the writing and the craft associated with writing it. They direct the students' attention to their modeling of the elements of the piece, often using think-alouds to share their thinking with students, so they can have a better understanding of the different elements of the piece and the writer's intent to include them all.

A teacher needs to be conscious of the craft of drafting a piece of work. As writers, we are constantly thinking and rethinking the way we want to organize our words, phrases, and ideas to best communicate our thoughts to the reader. When modeling, teachers need to bring this process alive for students, articulating the thought processes associated with effective writing and constantly engaging in a reflective process. They are thinking of the ideas, words, and phrases, as well as constantly refining the writing, searching for words, and reorganizing ideas in ways that would best represent the piece.

The prewriting stage allows students to think about the form of writing, explore other samples of the writing, and develop a solid understanding of the success criteria associated with it. Through the establishment of the success criteria, students are then able to reflect on their own writing and measure their progress in terms of it. As the writing continues, students are able to reflect on

Using mentor texts or exemplars during the prewriting stage assists students in developing a clear understanding of the things they will need to include in their writing to become more successful.

the success criteria and use the mentor texts, exemplars, or modeled pieces as a guide to shape their own work. The success criteria become the targets for the writing, and students are able to focus on this target as they begin to write and later revise their work. The success criteria are the agreed-upon set of skills that the teacher will use to provide feedback to students, and eventually use to assess their learning. This recursive writing process has students revisit their writing and continually reflect on ways to improve it; it is also recursive in that the success criteria that are developed in the early stages of writing continue to serve as the target for writing throughout the entire process. The success criteria are the constant beacon that helps guide students' writing and shape their learning.

Drafting: The Writing Process

During the drafting stage, the students are able to craft their own writing. There are a wide range of experiences that students may explore when experimenting with new forms of writing. Through this stage, the teacher can use various levels of support to assist students in the creation of their writing. This gradual release of responsibility helps students develop greater independence in a scaffolded approach. Some students work cooperatively with their peers, others need a little more support through a guided writing format, while others are ready to try working independently. The teacher will need to develop flexibility through this stage, and adapt the instruction to the differing needs of the students.

This is also the time when students might have differentiated opportunities surrounding their learning. Some students need access to technology, while others need a slightly different instructional approach—like chunking the writing into smaller, more manageable components. This is where teaching becomes a balance of science and art. As teachers, we become very adept at identifying which students can learn best in which circumstances. There are many different learning opportunities that can be provided to students to best support their various learning styles. As students are drafting their writing, we need to provide a classroom in which diversity is acceptable; although the students all strive toward the same success criteria, the route that each one takes to get there may be different. Writing is not necessarily an on-your-own-in-a quiet-corner activity—although for some it might be just that. Others might need the social atmosphere of sharing their ideas orally with their peers, or writing cooperatively through shared writing experiences. Finally, others might thrive while working in a small, focused writing group with an adult.

Regardless of the style of learning or the level of support, throughout their writing time students need to remain mindful of the success criteria that were carefully established in the prewriting stage. The success criteria guide the students' writing by outlining very clear expectations and targets. As the students begin to draft and reflect on their writing, having a clear understanding of the success criteria will help them to focus on the important aspects of their writing.

Revising and Editing: Using Descriptive Feedback

Once students have had the opportunity to explore the writing form and draft a piece, the teacher provides descriptive feedback. This feedback is crucial for students to move forward in the writing process. There is no purpose in providing feedback on completed writing pieces (once the student has published the piece), since there is no room for making improvements at that stage. The time

Through the drafting stage, we need to be aware of the different strategies and skills that students have, the wide range of interests and prior experiences they bring, and the areas with which they need support.

At this early stage in the writing process, it is easier to help students to think critically about their writing.

for feedback is after the student has created a draft, and before the student has created a finished piece.

Feedback can take many forms: individual or group conferences, written or oral response. Regardless of the form, the foundation for the feedback remains the success criteria. As students are able to measure their progress against the pre-established targets, they become more adept at identifying their areas of strengths and areas for improvement. When we provide students with feedback, they are then able to set goals for themselves and determine their next steps.

Some students might simply need to make some revisions to their writing—adding, deleting, or changing small portions of their work. Others might need to rework larger sections of text, inserting or reorganizing ideas to make the piece work more effectively. Others might wish to retry the writing, starting a new piece as a way of continuing or applying their learning. During this stage, students continue to reflect on the previous stages, using the mentor texts and success criteria as guides, and to plan their next steps.

Once again, the writing process seems much more complex than a linear process, and its recursive nature becomes evident. Through the various stages of writing, students and teachers are constantly reflecting on earlier stages and revisiting them in order to move forward. Using the success criteria, students are able to reflect on their proximity to reaching the targets set for the piece of writing. They are then able to refocus their attention based on the feedback provided from the teacher. Feedback assists them in setting their personal goals for improvement, moving forward while remaining focused on the success criteria.

Revising and editing are very different steps—during the revising stages, the piece is still being shaped, the ideas are being formed and the organization of the piece may be changing; editing is the process of polishing the writing and making it ready to share with others.

When a student chooses to take a piece of writing through to the final stages and produce a published version, it is important that it be edited carefully. When editing, the piece is made as correct as possible in terms of the conventions of writing: spelling, grammar, punctuation, capitalization, etc. Many students (and sometimes teachers) misinterpret the revising stage for editing. During the revising stage, the piece might change dramatically; during editing, the student is polishing the writing and making it ready to share with others. It is very disheartening for students when teachers mistake a writing conference for an editing session, filling the student's work with corrections. This extreme editing is not beneficial to anyone, and is often frustrating to both teacher and student. The students need to be taught effective editing strategies and learn to apply them to their own writing. This may include identifying words that "look funny" or reading sentences aloud to make sure that they "sound right." Students need to take charge of their editing, identifying areas that need correcting and finding strategies necessary to do so.

Not every piece needs to be edited, in the same way that not every piece needs to be published. As teachers, we need to think about what the students are getting from the process.

Teachers need to think about the learning that is intended from each writing task. Some students may benefit from writing a new piece in a similar form and having an opportunity to apply their learning to a new piece, rather than investing the time in editing and publishing the initial piece of writing. It is important that students publish some pieces of writing each term for the opportunity to share their work with others, as well as to develop the skills associated with editing. However, if students were to write three or four different pieces, and then select one to publish, this might yield greater learning and engagement than an insistence that every piece continue through the writing process to completion. Most students are excited by the prospect of starting a new piece and exploring their creativity with their writing, especially once they are certain of the success criteria.

Publishing: Sharing, Reflection, and Assessment

This final stage of the writing process includes sharing, reflection, and assessment of the student's writing. Students and teachers are able to measure the piece against the success criteria that were initially established. They can use the success criteria to form student-friendly rubrics that enable students to evaluate their work.

Students need to have a solid understanding of the success criteria, and use this as a basis for developing their writing. Success criteria form the foundation for feedback and revision. Finally, assessment of the students' writing is also based on the success criteria.

Throughout the entire writing process, students develop a very clear understanding of the areas that will be assessed through their writing, so it becomes easy for them to reflect on their learning in these terms. As teachers, we can use this stage not only to determine the students' levels of achievement, but also to guide our instruction. Through assessment, we become aware of which areas students have become proficient with, and which skills remain areas for continued growth. This reflective teaching is essential in order to continually build on students' successes and fill in the gaps that inadvertently develop.

This stage remains firmly rooted in the initial stages of the writing process, using the success criteria as the basis for assessment, and the exemplars or mentor texts as a guide for reflection and evaluation. Finally, when reflecting on the student's learning, it is helpful to also consider the feedback that was provided, and the ways in which the student tried to apply it to the work. It again becomes very clear that the writing process is not linear. Writers are constantly revisiting previous stages and rethinking about how to apply the learning to other steps in the writing. Students may choose to move from the revising stage back to the drafting stage many times before selecting a piece to move on through the editing and publishing stages, all while reflecting on the prewriting stage. The publishing stage is firmly grounded in the prewriting stage, but highly influenced by the revising stage. The revising stage also is firmly rooted in the prewriting stage, and may lead to the editing stage or back to the drafting stage. All this indicates that the writing process is one in which the steps are constantly intertwined and highly reflective.

Steps in the Assessment-Based Writing Process

Steps in the Assessment-Based Writing Process

1. Using Model Texts and Modeled Writing
2. Co-Constructing Success Criteria
3. The Writing Process
4. Conferencing and Coaching
5. Revising, Reworking, or Retrying
6. Assessment and Reflection

In the assessment-based writing process, students are given the opportunity to deconstruct mentor texts, exemplars, or pieces modeled by the teacher to determine the success criteria for the piece. The students then use the success criteria to guide their writing. As we know, the writing process is a recursive one—students write, revise, and then continue to write. In this light, students work to create a draft of their writing, revising and reflecting with the success criteria in mind as they work. The teacher uses descriptive feedback to guide the student in terms of the success criteria. The student is then encouraged to revise, rework, or retry the writing. Finally, with the assessment-based writing process, students are integral partners in setting the success criteria and using them as a means to determine the assessment and evaluation tools. Students are directly involved in creating the rubrics that will serve to assess their work. When students are active participants in the assessment process, they are more able to internalize and apply the skills and strategies necessary to meet with success.

The steps in the assessment-based writing process are, in fact, "The End." They represent the target, the outcome, the big picture. Using this framework as a guide, we will develop a deeper understanding of how each element works together to help youngsters become effective, reflective writers.

1. Using Model Texts and Modeled Writing

Exemplars and mentor texts can help students to understand and rationalize the different levels of achievement with a given form of writing. Students use these exemplars as a guide for determining the success criteria. Through modeled writing, students observe the processes and decisions we make as writers. Students discover that writing is a process, and that the process is just as important as the final product.

2. Co-Constructing Success Criteria

The success criteria make up a list of features that a successful piece of writing contains. Students can identify key features of the text form, content, style, word choice, personal connections, ideas, conventions, etc. Success criteria can be grouped according to specific categories: Knowledge (success criteria that demonstrate an understanding of the form of writing), Thinking (success criteria that show how creative ideas are included in writing), Communication (success criteria that pertain to conventions, voice, word choice, expression, sentence structure, and organization), and finally Application (success criteria that demonstrate students' application of their learning and personal connections to their writing). Developing success criteria with students ensures that students have a clear understanding of the elements of a successful piece of writing and how they all fit together.

3. The Writing Process

Through the writing process, students try out their understanding of the form of writing. They use the set of success criteria as a guide to focus their writing and ensure that they have included all the necessary elements. Through this process, teachers can use various elements of the gradual release of responsibility to coach students through their writing. It also becomes possible to explore countless opportunities for differentiating the activity to suit the needs of all learners.

4. Conferencing and Coaching

Once students have completed their first piece of writing, teachers can hold writing conferences to provide effective descriptive feedback. This feedback and the students' self-reflection focuses on measuring their work in relation to the target—through the success criteria. The feedback consists of mostly celebrations of the things students have done successfully, and includes one or two things to think about in order to improve their writing.

5. Revising, Reworking, or Retrying

Based on the descriptive feedback, students either revise and rework their piece of writing, or write another piece to apply and transfer their learning from the conference. The student and teacher work together to set goals for this new piece of writing.

6. Assessment and Reflection

Using the co-constructed success criteria, students collaborate with the teacher to create a rubric that will be used as a tool for assessment. This way, students have a very clear understanding of the different levels of achievement with respect to the success criteria that were created. Students engage in self-reflection, self-assessment, and goal-setting for future learning.

Four Influences on Writers

Four forces—Accessibility, Authenticity, Audience, and Assessment—provide the motivation and structure for all writing pieces. Writers need to know who they are writing to, the purpose for their writing, and the way in which it will be judged.

I confess to be a reluctant writer. Although I have completed and published three books, under most circumstances I hesitate to pick up a pen. I would rather commit important things to memory than mechanically record facts. I dread writing thank-you notes, and prefer to organize my ideas in what end up to be generally indiscernible graphic organizers. I am not typically a person who writes to reflect on my own practice or to resolve issues in my life. However, in the last few years I have become an avid writer—given the correct circumstances. I may hesitate to pick up a pen, but insist on thinking with a computer in front of me. My brain seems to have a direct connection to my fingers, which respond with the rhythmic tapping of keys, that the mechanical scrolling of a pen across a page just doesn't create. I am aware of the purpose and intent for my writing. I know that I am writing about something I firmly believe in, and know it is worth sharing with others. As a writer, I am constantly thinking about you. Yes, you—the reader. I envision you at your desk, sitting in your staff room, or comfortably lounging somewhere in your home, reading the words on the page and trying to make sense of the ideas and thoughts recorded therein. Finally, I recognize the challenges of putting together a good book. I think about how it will be judged, assessed, and reviewed. I consider the ways it will be measured against all of the outstanding literature, and wonder how I can ever begin to meet those high standards. Yes, I am a reluctant writer; however, I have four things that drive my writing: Accessibility, Authenticity, Audience, and Assessment. These are the four driving forces that serve to motivate, engage, and empower young writers.

Accessibility

Youngsters bring a full background of experiences, personal interests, and abilities to all learning tasks. Some students savor the craft of neatly scrolling their pencil on the page to construct beautiful letters, to form words, sentences, and articulate paragraphs. These students think of writing as the process of putting pen to paper, while others think of it as the formation of words, ideas, and images that convey information to the reader—regardless of the form it takes. In this rapidly changing world, technology is evolving faster than most of us can keep up. Older students converse in short snips of information, texting bursts of conversation from one end of the world to the other in seconds. They use a language full of acronyms and phrases that most adults fail to comprehend. We are training students now for jobs that do not yet exist—how can we support them in this? We need to think of writing as a means to convey information, setting the goals and the targets with the students, but providing as many different ways of creating the text as necessary.

When we think about how students will begin to record their ideas through the drafting stage and reflect on them through the revising stage, we need to be thoughtful about the different learning styles that students bring to our classrooms. Providing accessibility to writing tools for our young learners ensures that we consider technology another tool with which we can help our students reach their goals. Some students are eager to draft their ideas, neatly scribing their words across the page, whereas others need the various technology resources available to them. Although it would be wonderful to envision a world where laptops were available to all students who desired them, the reality is that there are few schools with those kinds of resources. However, if we begin by providing students with access to some of these tools at early ages, they become aware of the different approaches that one can take to writing and eventually develop a style that works best for them.

Perhaps we need to be less insistent that the letters fit between the lines and more aware of how the ideas fit the story. Teachers should be intuitive about the youngsters who struggle with fine motor coordination, about the ones for whom the act of writing a page is painfully tedious. We need to find ways for these youngsters to have access to writing, to recording their ideas for others to read. Engaging students with shared writing activities gives them the opportunity to share their ideas. Scribing for young students helps them begin to see themselves as competent authors with ideas worth sharing.

Given the right support, youngsters will find effective ways of composing their ideas, organizing their sentences, and filling the page with their voice. We just need to be flexible enough to recognize the various styles and preferences our youngsters bring to the table. This differentiation is important as we think of the different skill sets, interests, and prior experiences that students bring into our classrooms. Providing accessibility to a range of writing opportunities will assist students in becoming more reflective through the writing process, as they explore tools and strategies that allow them to practice their learning.

> Envisioning oneself as an author is the first step in becoming a capable, competent writer. We need to make a habit of referring to all young writers as authors. After all, what is an author? Someone who records their ideas for others to read. Aren't we all authors?

Authenticity

Before we start any piece of writing, our first question should be "What is the purpose of this piece of writing?" Writers need to know why they are writing a given piece of writing. How is it real? Why is it important? When we know that the work we are doing has true value, we are more likely to be engaged in it. Authenticity maximizes engagement.

Many years ago, I was a student in Grade 11 math class, and we were learning about drawing three-dimensional vectors in two-dimensional space. I sat, perplexed, at the back of the classroom. The teacher droned on for what seemed like hours on end. Finally, I voiced the thought that many of my classmates had but were afraid to ask: "Sir, when are we ever going to need this in the real world?" As his chalk dropped to the floor, all of my classmates' heads snapped to attention to hear his response. He slowly adjusted his glasses, and replied, "It will be on the final exam, so I suggest you pay attention." He returned to his confusing diagram with an X-, Y-, and Z-axis—leaving everyone to continue to stare in confusion at the array of lines drawn on the board. And to this day, I'm still not sure where the Z-axis goes.

Many years later, as an adult, I was given the opportunity to fly in the cockpit of an airplane. As I gazed around, I suddenly realized that the aircraft itself was a vector traveling in three-dimensional space, and the little blips on the two-dimensional radar screen marked our location. From the front of the plane I was able to see in all directions. I became aware of other aircraft in our vicinity, and suddenly comprehended the kind of situation in which one would need to know about three-dimensional vectors and their points of intersection! It became clear that there was a real-life purpose and application for the skills that were introduced so many years ago, and I hoped earnestly that my pilots had paid more attention in math class than I had. I now saw a purpose and value to that learning. I finally understood why it would be important to be able to track three-dimensional objects on a two-dimensional grid, and I certainly knew why it was important to be able to determine how and when these vectors might intersect. If my Grade 11 math teacher had been able to articulate a genuine purpose to the skill he was teaching, he would have had much more of the students' attention. We would have seen the value to it, and understood where we were going to need it in the real world.

Our young writers need to have a clear understanding of why they are writing. Through the process of exploring mentor texts, exemplars, and modeled writing, students are able to explore the authenticity of the text form. They are able to discover the key elements of the piece, and the purpose for which it is written. When students and teachers begin to deconstruct these texts and develop success criteria, the students are able to see the writing as purposeful and important. They are able to explore real-life applications to their learning, and they are more likely to be engaged in the task at hand.

As teachers, we need to make sure that we are providing authentic writing tasks that are engaging to our learners. Our students need to know that what they are writing has purpose, value, and authenticity. Youngsters need to see their learning as real and applicable to the world in which they live. In order to build their capacity as writers, they need to be engaged in the tasks at hand; in order to be fully engaged, they need to view their writing as important and authentic. When introducing new genres to students, it is imperative that we demonstrate clearly to them the connections the writing has to the world. They need to be able to identify when and where the form of writing would be needed, and have some experience interacting with authentic mentor texts in this style. When youngsters are honing their skills and developing their craft, they need to have a clear understanding of why they are learning the things that they are and of where they will need to apply their skills in the real world.

Audience

"Know your audience" is essential wisdom for anyone in public speaking or public relations. This is also true for authors. Writers need to consider the target audience for their piece of work. Would you write differently for children than colleagues? Would you write differently for an administrator than for the parents of the community? What about the differences between writing to a friend and a professional business acquaintance? The voice, tone, and form of our writing are greatly affected by the audience for whom it is intended.

Young writers need to identify the audience for their writing and to recognize that the words they put on the page will be read and interpreted by another person. David Booth speaks of teaching readers to think like writers, and writers to think like readers. Our youngsters need to envision themselves as authors, crafting a piece of text that will be read and interpreted by a reader. Having an audience for a piece of writing not only guides the direction of the writing, but

Consider the authenticity of surrounding students with favorite recipes, and then trying them out. This would provide students with much-needed prior knowledge of procedural writing, and greatly maximize their understanding of the authenticity of this text form. There is not a youngster alive who would not be eager to explore the elements of a text form if it meant that it would result in delicious food at the end.

also gives the writing value. Knowing that someone else will read it makes the writing authentic and purposeful. Young writers need to know that their words will affect someone—a friend, teacher, principal, or stranger. They need to think about the way in which they will phrase their ideas in order to have the greatest impact on their audience. Some casual phrases that might be suitable when writing to a friend might not be suitable when writing to a principal or for a larger audience.

Sometimes students need to recognize that the audience that they are writing for is themselves. Validating themselves as a suitable audience allows students to write for the pleasure of writing, for the skills of recording ideas to which they can later refer, and for the freedom to use writing as a way of expressing and working through their thoughts.

A Grade 6 math teacher was struggling to teach her students the concept of surface area, when she was confronted with the famous question; "When are we ever going to need this in the real world?" Her response was very different from that of the Grade 11 math teacher we met earlier. This creative teacher instructed all of her students to immediately check their lunches and find as many different varieties of drink boxes as they could. The teacher then set a task for the students to calculate the surface area of a juice box; then to find a shape that was able to hold the same amount of liquid, but with a smaller surface area. It didn't take long before all students had concluded that the cube was the shape with the least surface area but the maximum volume. Thinking of authenticity and audience, the teacher had her students write letters to all the different juice-box companies in an effort to convince them that the dimensions they had discovered were a better alternative for the product. The students discussed the various economic and environmental benefits of reducing the amount of cardboard needed to contain a volume of juice. These students knew their audience and wrote very persuasive letters to the companies. They recognized that their words would be read by others, and they were passionate about their writing. The letters were sent to the different companies and, believe it or not, some students actually received responses from companies about their products. One consumer who heard of their project started an online blog, outlining the project and invited many others to join in on the discussion.

When youngsters recognize that the words they write can influence others, their voice becomes powerful. When they realize that their audience is real and their writing is authentic, the purpose of their work is clear. The youngsters in that Grade 6 math class will never again question when and where they will need this math skill, and they found an audience for their writing that brought the realities of the world into the four walls of their classroom. Audience brings purpose and value to writing.

When we share mentor texts, exemplars, or modeled writing with students, we need to enable them to develop an understanding of the audience for the piece. Through the prewriting stage, students need to recognize the audience and voice of the sample texts. They might note this feature and include it in the success criteria. As students begin to draft their own pieces and reflect on them through the remainder of the writing process, they should reflect on the intended audience for the piece and consider how the writing can best serve to communicate with them.

Assessment

Assessment is the tool that guides our teaching practice and student learning. In order to know what to teach, we need to know where students are. In order for them to learn, they need to know where they are going.

Not long ago, a frantic shopper entered an unfamiliar shopping mall. In her urgency to locate the perfect gift for a teenage girl, she was in search of a specific item, from a specific store, in a specific color. As the shopper rushed into the mall, she was halted in her tracks by an onslaught of merchants equally competing for her attention. This savvy shopper headed straight for the oversized map of the mall. Gathering all of her focus, she squinted at the minuscule print that listed the stores in alphabetical order. She easily located the name of the specific store that was her target. She scanned the map and found the location of the shop on the far side of the mall. Placing her finger on the shop on the map, her eyes continued to search for the red "You Are Here" sticker. The consumer then began to make a mental note of the landmarks along the way to her desired location. She noted that she had to go down the escalator, turn left at the fountain, and then head straight through the food court. Turning her attention back to the store on the map, she also noted the larger shops that surrounded the specific store. In seconds, she had identified where she was going, where she was, what she needed to do to get to her goal, and what it would look like when she got there.

This is exactly the picture that assessment needs to paint for our students. They need to be able to clearly identify the target and explain where they are in relation to it. They need to know what they must do in order to get closer to the target, and what it will look like when they get there. Assessment-based learning ensures that students are active participants in the assessment and learning process; assessment and learning are not separate entities, but intimately interconnected. Assessment guides instruction, and instruction is based on the student's strengths and needs. Students' progress should be measured not only in terms of how close they are to the target, but also how far they have come from their initial location.

Throughout the assessment-based writing process, the students are constantly aware of the components that will be assessed in their writing. As they begin by deconstructing the sample texts, they are able to identify the success criteria that will serve to guide their writing. Their writing will be assessed using the success criteria as a way of measuring their learning. Using the success criteria as a basis for developing student-friendly rubrics ensures that students play an active role in their learning and assessment. As teachers discover students' strengths and needs through assessment, so too do students discover their strengths and set goals for their own learning.

There are three guiding questions (Stiggins, 2006) that surround assessment-based instruction: Where am I going? Where am I now? How can I close the gap? These questions are the underlying structure of the assessment-based writing process.

- As students begin to wonder "Where am I going?" the learning targets are clearly illustrated for them through the use of sample texts and the establishment of success criteria. When students are familiarized with the targets for the writing, they are able to have this goal firmly established from the beginning. Using exemplars allows students to see real-life samples of a range of levels of writing achievement, and to consider their targets.
- The second question can be answered two different times through the writing process. Once students have had the opportunity to draft a piece of work, they may use this writing as a basis for asking, "Where am I now?" The answer comes through conferencing and coaching, and the use of descriptive feedback—the teacher and student are able to reflect on the initial targets (success criteria) and measure the student's progress toward

applying them. Students may also reflect on this question at the final stages of the writing process, using assessment as a tool for reflection and further goal-setting. As students consider where they are in relation to the success criteria, they are able to continue to reflect on their learning, thinking about which skills they have managed to demonstrate and which continue to be areas for continued growth.

- The final foundational question for assessment-based learning is "How can I close the gap?" The answer to this question, like the answer to the second question, comes through the descriptive feedback and assessment provided by the teacher. As students become reflective, engaging in conferences with teachers and their peers, they can identify areas in which they need to continue to develop in order to further refine their writing. During the revising stage, the students can reflect on the specific piece of writing, measuring it in terms of the success criteria and setting goals for closing the gap with their work. Through assessment of a finished piece of writing, the teacher is able to further guide the student's learning by identifying specific areas that require continued growth and development. Through this assessment process, teachers are able to identify not only which areas their students' need to learn, but also which areas they themselves need to teach.

There are three guiding questions (Stiggins, 2006) that surround assessment-based instruction: Where am I going? Where am I now? How can I close the gap?

Assessment has two purposes—one for the student and one for the teacher: Students need to know where they are going, where they are, and what they need to do to get there. The teacher needs to know where the students are, where they are going, and what they need to get there. Ask yourself, "How are we going to teach them if we don't know where they are? And how are they going to learn if they don't know where they're going?"

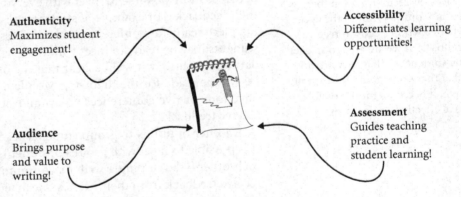

Authenticity
Maximizes student engagement!

Accessibility
Differentiates learning opportunities!

Audience
Brings purpose and value to writing!

Assessment
Guides teaching practice and student learning!

Balanced Literacy and Assessment-Based Writing

Fitting everything into a literacy block is a constant challenge. We all face the never-ending list of things we need to complete during a literacy block while the number of minutes remains the same. We are reminded of modeled reading, shared reading, guided and independent reading; we are told to add modeled writing, shared writing, guided writing, and independent writing. To this we add establishing success criteria and engaging in writing conferences to provide descriptive feedback. And to top it off, students should be reading for 30 to 40 minutes a day and writing for the same. There are not enough minutes in the school day, let alone the literacy block, to fulfill all these requirements.

Relax. The goal of a balanced literacy program is just that —to balance the needs of the students with the instruction that is being provided. That does not mean that we can forgo essential elements of a literacy program, but there are times when more time may need to be devoted to specific areas than others.

In effective balanced literacy, the independent times (independent reading and independent writing) become the backbone and foundation for the language block. These times have two main purposes: first, they allow the students time to practice, apply, and consolidate the skills that have been learned throughout the areas of instruction; second, they free up the teacher to be able to provide individual or small-group instruction. When students are working independently, they need to know that the work they are doing is valuable, authentic, and engaging. This is the only way to ensure that the independence is maintained. Although it may appear that independent work occurs on its own, and students should just know what to do, this is not the case. At the beginning of the year, it is crucial that teachers invest the time in developing solid independent reading and writing times so that students are aware of the expectations for these times. In this way, the teacher is able to provide small-group instruction for reading and writing on a daily basis. The most effective way to monitor and strengthen student learning is through regular ongoing small-group or individual instruction and feedback.

When facing the realities of a classroom, the challenge to find time to conference with all students becomes a difficult one to meet. One of the most effective strategies for overcoming this obstacle is by using flexible due dates for writing pieces. If students are given a flexible date as a target, some students will finish early, some will finish on time, and, of course, some will be late. If students are given the opportunity to sign up for writing conferences when they are ready, it becomes more possible to meet with everyone without students waiting days for their feedback. For example, if students are encouraged to have a draft of a writing piece ready for conferencing on Wednesday, then starting on Tuesday some students may be ready to meet with the teacher, some will be ready on Wednesday, and by Friday it will be clear that the ones who need the weekend to finish up will be ready for the following Monday. This way, the teacher will probably have four or five conferences a day, and no student needs to wait too long to receive feedback.

Another option is to group students according to their strengths and needs. It is possible to meet with groups of students and encourage them to share with each other—developing a writer's community where they are able to give and receive feedback from their peers. As teachers, we can group students into flexible writing groups for feedback and skill-building mini-lessons.

If we truly think of the writing process as recursive, then there is no end, only a point in the cycle where a writer needs to receive feedback. If we are able to stagger the students so that they are not all at that same point at the same time, it becomes more possible to have effective conferences.

CHAPTER 2

Using Model Texts and Modeled Writing

If you were given a car and a map, but not the essential information of your destination or end point, chances are that you would travel around aimlessly and, in all likelihood, never arrive at the desired location. This example may seem bizarre and far-fetched until we realize that, for some of our students, it is all too accurate a picture of their learning. They feel that they are navigating the concepts and teachings that are happening in their classrooms without knowing what the target is or what steps they must take in order to be successful at reaching the proper outcome. They have no concept as to the end point and what it should look like.

There is a good reason why puzzles always come in boxes with the final result, the picture of the finished puzzle, on the lid. The end point is there from the beginning for all to see and examine, before you even start working on assembling the puzzle. It is constantly there as you progress through the challenge. I doubt that there is anyone who has done an entire jigsaw puzzle without referring to the picture. It is not cheating; it is an effective strategy for being successful. Our students require the same courtesy. They need to see the end result before they can be expected to complete the task correctly. In order to truly begin with the end in mind, both teachers and students need to have a clear vision of where that end is. We need to be able to examine its components and articulate the elements about it that makes it correct.

As a way of bringing learning targets into focus for students, teachers may find mentor texts, student exemplars, and teacher modeling valuable tools. We can use them as a vehicle to deconstruct the learning and establish the elements that make it possible and successful—the success criteria.

> As teachers, we need to have a clear understanding of the targets we need to set for our students. We need to ensure that our instruction and assessment are firmly based on the specific curriculum expectations set out for each grade. As we move from year to year, our program will reflect the diverse needs of each group of students while our foundation remains in the curriculum and assessment guidelines.

Exemplars and Mentor Texts

In the initial stages of the writing process, students need ample time to become familiar with the form of writing and the expectations of the task. They need the time to explore samples of good writing and develop an understanding of the elements that make it successful. Establishing a set of criteria for success enables students to have a clear purpose and target for their own writing. Students can construct success criteria based on a number of different sample texts. Teachers can use exemplars, mentor texts, or modeled writing to develop students' understanding of the writing task.

> Through the prewriting stage of examining model texts, students develop a clear understanding of the elements of the piece, the style with which it is written, and the way in which it will be assessed.

Exemplars

Exemplars are samples of student work. Students love being able to "play the teacher" and deconstruct a piece of writing that has been written by another student. However, in order to develop an environment in which students are encouraged to take risks and explore their own writing, exemplars should not be taken from the current group of students.

It is important to use exemplars written by anonymous students. This removes any element of bias or subjectivity.

There are two different approaches that teachers may use to begin to deconstruct exemplars with students: students can rank, order, and justify their choices from a range of levels of samples; or they can identify the successful features of a number of different high-level samples.

Ranking Exemplars

In the first instance, students are provided with a range of samples. The writing samples would include strong and weak examples of writing. Working with partners or in groups, students rank the writing pieces from weakest to strongest. As they do this, they will automatically engage in dialogue about why one piece is stronger than the other. Encourage students to capture these reasons and use them as a point for discussion with the whole class to establish success criteria. Once students have ranked the pieces, encourage them to share with the class their rationale and record their thinking as it pertains to what makes each piece strong or what a piece is lacking to make it weak.

This is a good time to point out that presentation and use of conventions might highly influence the students' impression of writing. They may think that a piece that is typed should score higher than a piece that is written by hand. They may think that a piece that has many spelling errors should be considered a poor writing sample because of the writer's lack of facility with writing conventions. This is a difficult point to convey to students—especially since most teachers are also greatly influenced by these features in writing. We need to look for the richness of ideas, use of personal connections, and application of the text form. If we are truly trying to get to the heart of the writing, we need to consider the deeper message of the text, the voice of the author, and the style of the writing, as well as the surface features of conventions and presentation.

We acknowledge that presentation and conventions do influence the reader, and we need to include them as elements in the success criteria; however, students (and teachers) need to look beyond the surface elements and delve deeper into the writing.

Keep in mind the intended learning for the group of students and ask guiding questions that will assist students in coming to a common understanding of the piece. For example, when exploring exemplars of a report, the teacher may draw the students' attention to key features by asking them to notice the way the ideas have been organized; to identify which supporting evidence is most effective; to note what style (voice) the writer used, how the introduction and conclusion are used to present the main idea of the piece, etc. By scaffolding the students' thinking while exploring exemplars, we are able to assist them in coming to the desired conclusions. This inductive form of instruction is highly effective, since students feel like they have "discovered" the keys to success, rather than having been told.

As students share their rationale and the discussion continues with the larger group, you will be able to work together to sort the different success criteria under the four areas of learning: Knowledge, Thinking, Communication, Application (see Chapter 3). This way, we are ensuring that there is a balance between areas of learning. Should the students note that most of their success criteria fall under one category, encourage them to think more about the other features that made the writing effective.

Using High-Level Exemplars

A second way of using exemplars to develop success criteria involves using only high-level samples of work. We provide peers, or groups of three or four, different samples that are all considered high-level writing. Students look for the different features of each piece that make it successful. They might note that one piece has exceptional voice, whereas another has creative ideas. They might see that one includes detailed evidence, whereas another has skillfully applied knowledge of a text form. Students might be able to connect to a writer through that writer's words and develop empathy or anger toward different characters. As the groups of students discover the different ways they can deconstruct the samples, encourage them to write on sticky notes or use margin notes to record the different features they have found.

Once students have had ample time to explore the exemplars, the whole class should engage in a rich discussion about the different exemplars and the features that made each a high-level sample. As students share, record their ideas for all to see, or place their sticky notes on chart paper as a way of collecting ideas from everyone. As the ideas are collected, they may be categorized into the four areas of learning (Knowledge, Thinking, Communication, Application; see Chapter 3), ensuring a balance between all four.

The collection of ideas will serve as the basis for developing the success criteria for the piece. As the teacher collects and records the students' ideas, it is possible to point out specific features of the piece, and discuss the way the author included them in the writing. For example, when examining exemplars of narrative writing, the teacher might ask: "Did you notice how the writer used foreshadowing to create suspense?" or "Which exemplar had the strongest example of visual imagery?" In this way, the teacher is assisting the students in recognizing the key features that will become the focus for their own writing, their feedback, and their assessment.

Mentor Texts

A mentor text can be any piece of written work: a picture book by a favorite author, an article in the newspaper, a report that was posted on the Internet, or a letter that may have been included in a text book.

Mentor texts can serve as a vehicle in the development of success criteria. A mentor text can be any piece of writing that clearly demonstrates the high levels of success in the skills that we are striving to develop in our students. It needs to include recognizable text features and clear ideas. It should be at an appropriate level for students to read and try to emulate, as well as being of a manageable length. For example, a report from a science text would be a suitable mentor text, as would a letter to the editor in the newspaper. However, a mystery novel or a thesis paper would not: the first is much too long, and the other much too complex. Students need to access texts that are short, effective, and clear. Using texts that are too long or complicated will limit the students' ability to remain focused on their task—not only reading and understanding the text, but analyzing and articulating the elements of it.

With peers or in groups, students should explore the features of the mentor text. Encourage them to record the things they notice about it that make it an effective piece of writing. Which text form did it follow? What are the text features the author used effectively? How did the author develop ideas? How did the author use descriptive writing and clear evidence to support his/her work? What was the author's main message? How did the author make that clear?

What connections did the author make through his/her writing? What research do you think the author did to write this piece? …and the list goes on.

Once the students have had sufficient time to record their ideas, the discussion with the whole class will be rich with their observations. As they share the features that they noticed in the mentor text, group the features into the four areas of learning (Knowledge, Thinking, Communication, Application; see Chapter 3), ensuring a balanced focus for instruction and assessment.

While students are exploring the mentor texts or sharing their observations, we can scaffold students' thinking by asking thoughtful questions. For example, while students are reading mentor texts by favorite children's author Robert Munsch, encourage them to notice how he uses repetition to draw the reader's attention to an important event or item. When exploring letters to the editor, encourage students to identify the main idea and the call to action of the letter. When examining a procedure (like a recipe), ask students to note the way the steps of the process are recorded. Through this prewriting, the students are developing a familiarity with the text form and are able to set the targets for their own writing.

As students generate the success criteria, we need to ensure that the criteria are realistic, accurate, and relevant. The students may notice things about the piece, but if they are not intentional foci for student learning, acknowledge them but do not include them on the list of success criteria. For example, a student notes that all of the subtitles of a report are alliterations; although this may be an interesting coincidence, it is not a feature that should be listed in the success criteria.

Modeling

Teacher modeling is an essential component in developing strong writers. As teachers we need to be able to demonstrate to our students the strategies that we use as writers, our thoughts, and the way we overcome our challenges. Through this process, we need to model writing pieces that are authentic and strong samples of writing. If we want our students to write with voice, then we need to include it in our own writing. If we want them to take risks and stretch their vocabulary, then we need to demonstrate strategies for finding new words or sounding out the ones we don't know how to spell. Our writing must be authentic and rich with the skills we are asking our students to emulate.

Teacher modeling is an important part of the writing process. It is a part of the gradual release of responsibility, and also assists students in developing a good understanding of the craft of writing. The piece that is produced through teacher modeling can serve as a basis for developing success criteria with students. As students watch the teacher craft the piece, they are able to hear the thought processes associated with writing, and they are able to identify the elements associated with the text form.

Using think-aloud during the writing process gives students greater insight into the intentionality of how the words are written on the page. For example, the teacher might say: "I'm going to try to create the element of suspense, so I'm going to use short sentences to get the reader to read quickly"; or "I think I'll use foreshadowing by giving the reader a hint of what's to come"; or "I want the reader to be able to visualize this section, so I'm going to describe it really

After teacher modeling, students can use the completed piece of writing as a mentor text, deconstructing it to establish success criteria. Students can identify the various text features, skills, and strategies that are demonstrated through the piece. They can note the use of form, ideas, conventions, and connections that the teacher has made through writing.

vividly." This opportunity for the students to observe a writer at work enables them to understand the craft involved in producing a piece of writing.

Students can jot their ideas down on sticky notes and stick them on the teacher's modeled piece, or the teacher can highlight areas of the writing that demonstrate specific skills that the students need to notice. As students identify these successful features, they can be grouped into the four areas of learning (Knowledge, Thinking, Communication, Application; see Chapter 3) to ensure that a balance is being made between all areas.

As we model, we can draw the students' attention to the various elements that will become important in their own writing. As we construct the success criteria with the students, we are able to engage in a dialogue with them about which strategies we used to get the desired effect, and what we were thinking about while crafting the piece. This insight into a writer's mind is important for young authors, to whom writing seems somewhat of a mystery. They need to recognize that the words do not just magically appear on the page; a piece of writing is the result of an internal dialogue and reflective thought process that the writer uses to find just the right word or phrase, to organize ideas so that they are clear to the reader.

The establishment of success criteria targets three of the four influences on a writer: Authenticity, Audience, and Assessment. As students and teachers begin the writing process by becoming familiar with the expectations of the writing task, the authenticity of the writing becomes clear. Using mentor texts provides students with real-life applications for the writing skills that they are learning. They are able to clearly see the purpose and application for their writing, so their engagement is heightened. Through the use of the different sample texts, the students are able to identify the audience for the various pieces, and to consider the audience for their own writing. As they begin the drafting stage, they have had the opportunity to consider possible audiences for writing and to think about the intended audience for the sample texts that they read. Finally, as the students explore the different sample texts and establish the success criteria, they are developing the targets for their learning, as well as the tools with which they will be assessed. Using the success criteria as a basis for descriptive feedback and as a foundation for student-friendly rubrics ensures that students have a clear understanding of the assessment process from the start.

The setting of success criteria relates to the three guiding questions of assessment based learning: Where am I going? Where am I now? How can I close the gap? It is crucial to the first question: Where am I going? Through this initial exposure to sample texts and the development of the success criteria, students develop a clear understanding of where they are going. This understanding is key to the students being able to successfully apply their learning to their own writing. In order to include the success criteria in their writing, they need to have a clear understanding of what it looks like in the writing of others.

The Gradual Release of Responsibility

The gradual release of responsibility is the most effective way of enabling students to develop new skills. It relies heavily on the teacher as a model, mentor, and coach. This is not a new concept. It is something that we tend to do naturally when teaching youngsters a new skill. Only recently have we become cognizant of this process and effectively applied it to maximize student learning in the classroom.

Have you ever taught a youngster to tie his shoelaces? Chances are that you used the gradual release of responsibility. At the beginning, we show the youngster the steps involved in tying shoes. We start by saying, "Watch me: first this one goes over the other, then it goes underneath." While we are demonstrating the process, we are articulating the steps we are taking. Once the child has watched and listened to us, he is ready to try it out with some support. As his mentor, we gently guide his hands as he clumsily loops the laces together. We encourage, guide, and correct as necessary. There may be moments during this time when we need to untie a knot or help tighten a bow. We may actually hold the youngster's hands and guide them through the process of putting one lace over the other, then pulling tight. With this high degree of support, the youngster is able to meet with success. Finally, we take a step back and say, "Now you try it." The child is able to try it out on his own; however, we remain vigilant as a coach on the side, willing to support, advise, and guide as necessary. During this stage the youngster might struggle, get frustrated, end up with a giant knot—or, remarkably, meet with success. If we are available to coach and encourage him, he will quickly gain the confidence to try it again, and soon be a completely independent shoelace tier.

When we are teaching students a new skill, whether it be lace tying or writing, we need to go through a process of releasing the control and responsibility to the student. In the first stage of skill acquisition, students need to have a strong model from which to learn. They need to see the process in action and develop a complete understanding of the desired outcome. They also need to hear the steps described in, or the thinking that is involved with, each new stage of the task. As models, we need to ensure that we are providing our students with a complete picture of the process and the product. During this stage we are modeling the skill and providing a framework for their learning. We are providing the target that they will strive to achieve on their own.

During the second stage, we move from being model to mentor. This is our opportunity to support students as they begin to try it on their own. This intermediary stage, between our modeling a skill and students independently performing it, is the most important. It provides us with insight as the students begin to experiment with their new learning, allows us to identify any misunderstandings, and lets us gently nudge them in the direction of success. For students, it provides the opportunity to take risks, and gives them reassurance, encouragement, and direction while they know that we are supporting them.

During the final stage—independence—students have full ownership of their skills. But we remain vigilant, working as coach to continue to support and guide as necessary. If we think back to the shoelace-tying analogy, students will rely heavily on their prior experiences to determine how they will handle successes, challenges, or frustrations that may arise. If we continue to actively coach them during this stage, they will continue on their journey of learning, constantly refining their skill with our guidance.

As we move through the assessment-based writing process, we use varying levels of support in the prewriting and drafting stages. During the prewriting, teachers may use modeled writing as a way of establishing success criteria with the students, or as a way of illustrating the craft and strategies associated with the writing task. As students begin to draft their own pieces, the teacher needs to move from the role of model to mentor and coach, guiding the writing with varying levels of support as necessary. During the drafting stages, some students might require continued support in the form of guided-writing or shared-

When we are modeling, it is important to remember that the product and processes that we demonstrate and articulate to our students during the initial stage of skill acquisition will become their target.

By the third stage of skill acquisition, students have had enough previous experiences to become independent, relying on the teacher only for encouragement, guidance, and feedback.

writing experiences in order to begin to feel comfortable with the text form. Other students may be ready to move to a more independent form of writing, trying it out on their own. The gradual release of responsibility illustrates the different levels of support that students might need in order to become comfortably independent with writing.

Modeled Writing

The teacher models effective writing to students by recording the words while thinking aloud, demonstrating problem-solving skills and strategies. All students need to be able to see the text as it is created.

Modeled writing works best as a large-group instructional format. You might choose to use modeled writing as a means of creating a mentor text that students can deconstruct in order to identify the success criteria. Construct the piece while the students observe, then use guiding questions to draw their attention to specific features within the piece. By identifying and labeling the different parts, the students are able to recognize not only the features, but how they all fit together to form a unified piece of writing. You might also use this as an opportunity to draw the students' attention to other parts of the writing, such as the voice, sentence fluency, and creative ideas.

An alternative way in which modeled writing might be used is to demonstrate to students how a writer may incorporate success criteria into a piece of writing. In this case, students and teacher first use mentor texts or exemplars to determine the success criteria for the piece. If the students have used a range of exemplars to determine the success criteria, post the success criteria and refer to them frequently while modeling the writing. Say something like, "I know that a good narrative includes descriptive writing, so I'm going to make sure that I describe the villain with lots of detail so that the reader can really picture him in their mind"; or "I want to make sure that my ideas are really connected together, so I'm going to use a linking phrase to make this clear to the reader." In this way, modeling is being used as a tool to demonstrate to the students the cognitive processes associated with writing with the success criteria in mind.

Shared Writing

In shared writing, teacher and students work together to create a piece of writing. The teacher controls the writing, but incorporates the students' ideas, words, and suggestions. The teacher also demonstrates thinking-aloud while writing. This may be completed with a small group or the whole class.

Some students enjoy working with their peers, cooperating to write a shared piece together. As students explore the text form, using the success criteria as a guide, they are able to rely on their friends for support, and they get creative inspiration and excitement from each other.

Guided Writing

In guided writing, the teacher works with a small group of students to guide them in applying strategies to their own writing. The students are grouped according to a specific instructional focus.

Shared- and guided-writing experiences may provide additional support for some students who are not quite ready to try it out on their own. Once the success criteria for a task have been determined, select a small group of students who may need just a little more support to incorporate the skills into their own writing. When you select a group for a guided- or shared-writing experience, it provides these students with the security they need to feel comfortable applying their new learning to their writing.

Independent Writing

In independent writing, students are given the opportunity to write on their own about a topic that has been assigned, or one of their own choosing. Create opportunities for students to write a range of text forms, genres, and formats.

There is no hard and fast way to use the gradual release of responsibility for students to move from the prewriting to the drafting stage of the writing process. Various approaches to supporting learners should cater to individual student needs, as well as provide a range of learning opportunities. Students enjoy having some variety in their routine, so incorporate a range of writing experiences for all students. For example, with one text form you might use the modeled piece to determine success criteria, and in the next writing task use modeled writing to illustrate how to incorporate the success criteria into the writing. In one task, you might determine the success criteria with students, then move to independent writing, selecting some students to work within a more focused guided-writing format; in a subsequent writing task, you might encourage the students to write cooperatively with their peers as they begin to incorporate the success criteria into their work. The options are limitless, as the students become familiar with using success criteria to guide their writing.

Authentic Modeling

When modeling writing to students, there are two elements to consider: the craft and the product. We need to ensure that we are providing students with an accurate target upon which to model their writing, as well as demonstrating an authentic craft of writing. They need to watch as we produce a piece of work that follows a specific form of writing, includes specific organizational strategies, and conveys the message it was intended to convey. On the other hand, they need to see that writers take risks, get excited at finding just the right word, experiment with the sounds that different words and phrases make together, and explore ways to strengthen their voice and purpose in writing. David Booth (2001) describes modeled writing as a collaborative process with his students: "I talk out loud in front of them using transparencies and charts, revealing how I revise and rethink my work as it develops, make decisions, edit the conventions—how I write down my life."

Hence, the craft and product are equally valuable for our young writers, and neither can be as effective in the absence of the other.

Modeling for Craft

Too often, when students watch a teacher write, attention is focused on the product rather than the authentic craft of writing. Usually the result of teacher modeling is a beautifully written composition, picture-perfect not only in appearance but also in conventions, ideas, and organization. One is reluctant to display a piece of teacher writing that has words crossed out, arrows indicating insertions and deletions, or reorganizations. Typically when modeling, teachers easily select words from their vocabulary, organize their ideas into smooth flowing sentences, and underline the title with multicolored markers and a ruler (or a decorative wavy line). When we model writing like this to our students, we are teaching students that writing is simple and clear, that our first draft is perfect, and that there is no need to take risks as a writer. Students get the impression that writing should be easy, beautiful, and correct the first time. This false perfection often results in feelings of frustration and inadequacy when students fall far short of this unrealistic target.

The truth about writing is very different. The act of writing creatively is a messy one. Students need to see the struggles we face as writers; they need to witness the challenges we overcome and the frustration that sometimes comes with writing. They need to observe a competent writer making decisions about writing, reworking ideas, and finding creative solutions to problems. They need to watch us taking risks, using words that stretch our vocabulary (even words for which we are unsure of the spelling), and struggling to find just the right phrase to capture our feelings. They need to watch us rework our sentences so that they flow smoothly together and capture the feeling of the piece. Students need to observe as we reorganize, delete, insert, and reorder ideas so that the purpose of the piece is more accurately conveyed.

Chances are that the writing that is produced through this type of modeling is not beautiful. But it is authentic. When students witness the authentic craft of writing, they are more likely to develop strategies that will help them to take greater risks as writers, to rework ideas that are not coming together, and to find creative solutions to their writing dilemmas. They become aware that they are not alone with the frustrations they feel with their writing, and that, in fact, these are challenges that all writers face.

Modeling for Product

When we model our writing, we need to ensure that we are providing students with an authentic perspective on the craft of writing. However, as writing teachers, our job is to ensure that our young writers end up with a clear vision of the features of writing we are teaching them. Regie Routman (2005) states "I always tell the story first before I write it. Saying the story out loud engages the students, lets me clarify my thinking, and reinforces the importance of conversation before writing."

Knowing that the product is vitally important, we need to ensure that before we begin, we ourselves, as writers, have a clear picture of the end product we intend to create. We need to predetermine how our writing will be organized, the purpose for the piece, and audience for whom it is intended. We need to pre-establish the elements we will include and think about the writing traits we wish to focus on. None of this happens incidentally. It requires conscious thought, so that our instruction may be purposeful and intentional.

The Teacher as Writer

Encouraging students to become reflective writers is a huge undertaking. We are asking them to become consciously aware of the strategies and skills that they apply to their work. In order to become reflective, one must truly be aware of one's own learning and thinking. It is our job as teachers to assist young writers in this journey of taking their writing to the next level. We need to teach them to become conscious of the decisions they make as writers, and of the skills and strategies they apply to strengthen their work. They need to have a clear vision of what good writing looks like; more importantly, they need to understand the components of a successful piece and how they all fit together. Moving from a

"When you begin to trust what you do as a writer, you will become a better writing teacher. You will notice that writing is recursive, not linear… That is, as we write, we continue to plan or pre-write, draft, make changes as we reread, edit as we go along, all in the process of getting our thoughts down." — Regie Routman, *Writing Essentials*

"[Writing is] pulling out all of the stops—recreating conversations, slowing down the writing with carefully chosen descriptive words, letting students in on my thinking and what I'm feeling." — Regie Routman, *Writing Essentials*

It is the metacognition of writing —thinking about the thinking processes involved with successful writing—that we want to develop. Students cannot learn from a process unless they are cognitively aware of the skills involved in it.

mechanical level of writing to a critical and thoughtful process is a challenge. Students need to be able to identify characteristics found in good writing, and develop an understanding of how to apply these to their own work.

Through the past few years, we have become very aware of the process of thinking aloud, especially in the area of reading. When this teaching strategy was introduced, it took many of us a long time to become comfortable with interrupting our reading, pausing, and explaining to students the thought processes happening in our heads. We needed to slow down and analyze the process we, as effective readers, went through to make sense of written material. This approach to teaching reading strategies has become a common and integral component of teaching students to become reflective readers. Now, with ease, students pause to discuss connections or predictions they have made, they share inferences and questions with each other, and they synthesize material, thinking critically about it and integrating it with their existing knowledge. This has been an incredible journey in the teaching world.

As we begin to transfer the learning we have developed around teaching reading strategies to writing, the first step is that we, as teachers, must become consciously aware of the thought process involved with writing. We must go beyond the literal level of writing; we must pause and think about our thinking as writers. We must become consciously aware of the decisions we make, the strategies we try, and the skills we apply to our writing—in order to articulate them to our students. We need to struggle with our word choice, refine our sentences to find the best flow, read aloud our writing and listen to the way it sounds to find our voice in our work. We need to experiment with various forms of writing, to search for our intent as writers and clearly define the purpose in the piece we are writing. This is by no means an easy task.

Here is a challenge for you: In order to become proficient at teaching writing, first you must become a proficient writer yourself. Would you take driving lessons from someone who has not driven for the 15 years since he was in high school? Would you learn to operate a table saw from someone who was afraid of loud noises? Would you learn to cook from a food critic who eats the food, or would a better choice for an instructor be the chef, the one who prepares it? As teachers, we need to reflect on our own journey as writers. When was the last time that you wrote creatively—something other than report cards? When was the last time that you paused to think about how you were going to convey an important message or point of view? When did you last take the time to articulate a persuasive perspective? When was the last time you wrote a report? The possible answer to all these questions: not since you were a student yourself. Is that the last experience you are drawing upon to teach your students to become reflective in their own writing?

We are being unfair to our young learners if we do not practice and reflect on the skills that we are trying to teach them. If we truly desire to teach effective writing, we must discover what we need ourselves to become effective writers. We cannot in good conscience teach students to write a piece of work that we ourselves have not had recent experience writing. Too often as teachers we become the food critic, identifying the success or failure of a piece of work based on the final product. Instead, we need to become the chef, developing a thorough understanding of all of the ingredients and how they work together to form the final product. Only the chef can alter a recipe to best suit her needs, and only teachers who write themselves are able to articulate the thinking processes involved in writing and develop this in their students.

Teaching students to become reflective readers has relied on our learning as teachers. Before we can share our thinking with our students, we must become consciously aware of it ourselves. Herein lies the challenge.

"You are a writer. Envision yourself as a writer" — Regie Routman, *Writing Essentials*

This is not an easy challenge. We recognize the many time constraints of a busy teacher, but the time you invest in developing your own strengths and overcoming your challenges as a writer will greatly pay off in the knowledge you will be able to share with your students. In the words of Regie Routman (2005), "If you have never written in front of your students before, take the plunge: they will appreciate your risk taking, and you will have a much clearer idea of what you are actually asking them to do." The next time you write, take the time to think about your writing, reflect on your writing process, and find a way to articulate your learning.

CHAPTER 3 *Co-Constructing Success Criteria*

Success criteria are the sets of skills that can be demonstrated through a piece of work. These are the indicators of success in a piece of writing. When we establish criteria with students, they are more likely to understand what is expected of them and to have personal ownership in the process.

We all seem to be able to recognize a good piece of writing when we come across one. But are we able to articulate exactly what it is about the writing that makes it good? Are we fascinated by the writer's use of descriptive imagery or the creative ideas behind the story? Is it the writer's voice and personality coming through in the writing that has caught our attention? Has the writer been able to engage and capture the reader's attention through interesting word choice or surprising elements? Perhaps writers have provided us with some deeper insight into themselves or helped us to empathize with a situation that is near and dear to their hearts. How do we begin to define these "good" qualities with success criteria that are tangible and measurable? We need to provide students with high-level samples of writing, and have them begin to articulate what they find appealing about them. In this way, students will begin to see authentic ways of integrating a range of writing strategies, and begin to think, "I see what the author is doing and what effect it is creating. I am going to try to do this too."

As we begin to set success criteria with students, it is important that we remember that the purpose of success criteria is to create a set of learning targets. The success criteria need to be reflective of the skills we are actively teaching them. The process of constructing success criteria is a joint one, but the teacher needs to remain cognizant of the learning goals set out for the class and partner with the students in defining them as learning targets.

Success criteria need to be balanced to reflect a complete picture of a successful piece of writing. Too frequently, students and teachers place a great deal of emphasis on conventions, neglecting to adequately develop the other areas of effective writing.

As a basis for developing success criteria, you can use a range of sample texts to help students identify the key features and learning targets, including exemplars, mentor texts, or teacher-modeled writing (see Chapter 2). Regardless of the type of sample text, it is important that students have sufficient exposure to the text form to develop a solid understanding of the style and elements associated with it. They need to develop their familiarity with the features of the text if they are to include them in their own writing.

The establishment of success criteria is the essential step in the assessment-based writing process. Through the examination of sample texts, students are able to develop a clear understanding of the expectations of the writing task. They are able to develop a set of targets that they will strive to include in their own writing, and that will serve to measure their success. This set of success criteria will also assist students in revising their writing, determining which skills they have used successfully and which ones they need to revisit. Using the list of student-constructed success criteria to create a student-friendly rubric ensures that students have a clear understanding of the ways in which their work will be assessed. Setting the success criteria through the use of sample texts answers the question "Where am I going?" by clearly illustrating to students "This is where you are going, and this is what it looks like!"

Grouping the Success Criteria

Most success criteria can be grouped into the following four areas of learning: Knowledge, Thinking, Communication, and Application (adapted from *The Ontario Curriculum Grades 1–8, Language*, 2006).

There are four areas that success criteria can be grouped into: Knowledge, Thinking, Communication, and Application. In short, Knowledge reflects the students' understanding of the form of writing (e.g., a narrative includes a setting, characters, and a plot), Thinking reflects the students' ideas (e.g., the plot is well-developed and has an exciting climax), Communication reflects the students' ability to express their ideas (e.g., voice, sentence fluency, spelling, etc.), and Application reflects the students' ability to connect their writing to their own experiences (e.g., the setting of the narrative is described as being just like the forest behind the student's house). As students and teachers begin to construct success criteria, it is important that there is a balance between these four areas of learning.

As students begin to deconstruct pieces of writing, you will find that the success criteria will fall into the four areas of learning. In order to develop a holistic approach to writing instruction and assessment, there needs to be a balance between the four areas to ensure that students become well-rounded writers. The four areas of learning become an important focus throughout the entire writing process, but are mostly crucial throughout the prewriting, revising, and assessment stages. As we establish success criteria with students, we need to ensure that there is a balance between the four areas of learning. When we provide feedback to students, it is important that we consider all areas of learning, and provide them with feedback that focuses on the specific area that is most important for them to strengthen. When assessing and evaluating students' work, it is important that we think of the writing as a complete piece, and judge the four areas in a balanced way.

Knowledge: What You Write

In this context, knowledge generally refers to the knowledge the writer has about the form of writing. This is the way writers use the different elements of a piece to develop and express their ideas. For example, students recognize that, when writing a persuasive piece, they need to include a strong opinion followed by supporting evidence and a call to action. If they are able to integrate the important features of a specific form of writing, then they have demonstrated their knowledge of writing.

Thinking: What You Say

Thinking represents students' ideas. It is the richness of creativity that students bring to the piece. It is the creative and critical process of determining which ideas are important to convey the message of the piece. Through their thinking, students develop their ideas, organizing their thoughts so they flow in a logical and sequential process and are clear for the reader. For example, two students may write narratives; however, one may be about the mundane events of an everyday soccer game, while the other may be about the adventures of a child spy. The richness of the thinking comes with the development of the ideas that the writer brings to the piece. Both narratives might have the important elements of the text form (setting, characters, and plot), but one may be much stronger in ideas, or thinking, than the other.

Communication: The Way You Say It

Communication is the area of writing that demonstrates the way the ideas are expressed. This includes the use of voice, word choice, sentence fluency, and adherence to writing conventions. It is the way the author is able to communicate ideas to the reader. When students are effective in communicating their writing, they are able to consider the audience for the piece, to select appropriate words, and to organize their ideas into smooth flowing sentences and paragraphs. As a part of effective communication, students need to ensure that their spelling, grammar, and punctuation are conventionally correct.

Application: The Way You Connect to It

As writers, we bring our prior experiences and knowledge to each writing piece. We are able to determine which text form is best suited for which purpose. We are able to apply our understanding of how writing works to make our writing stronger. It is through the application area of learning that students are able to demonstrate their connections to the world. Students are able to illustrate their writing with rich connections to facts or personal experiences that give the reader a sense of the author's world.

Establishing and Using the Success Criteria

Teachers can use a range of tools (including using mentor texts, exemplars, and teacher modeling) to develop success criteria with their students; see Chapter 2. Students are given the opportunity to deconstruct high-level samples of work and determine the features that make them effective.

As teachers and students begin to co-construct success criteria, they can arrange them into the various areas of learning and write them into student-friendly target statements. Students may find it helpful to record the success criteria in terms of "I will…" or "My writing includes…" This way, when students reflect on their writing, they are able to indicate whether they remembered to include, or will continue to think about, a particular skill.

Consider the following sets of success criteria that were developed for a narrative writing task. The success criteria for a piece will differ depending on the level of the students. The chart on page 37 shows sets of success criteria for students in Grade 2 and Grade 6. Many of the key concepts remain the same; however, the level of sophistication changes as the students age. Although the task is similar, the difference between expectations for the different grades can be seen through the success criteria.

Sample Success Criteria: Narrative	
Grade 2 Success Criteria	**Grade 6 Success Criteria**
Knowledge: What I Write • I will write a story that has realistic characters and places. • I will include a problem in my story. • I will include (three) events in the story that lead to a solution. • I will have an ending that tells the solution.	**Knowledge: What I Write** • I will include the elements of a narrative (setting, characters, and plot). • The plot development will include a clear climax and resolution.
Thinking: What I Say • I will have exciting ideas that the reader will want to read. • I will organize the events in my story in a way that makes sense.	**Thinking: What I Say** • I will use descriptive writing. • My narrative will be logical and make sense. • I will include enough information to make the story fit together
Communication: The Way I Say It • I will include feelings in my story. • I will use important connecting words (*and, then, because*). • I will leave spaces between the words; I will use capitals at the beginning of sentences and periods at the end.	**Communication: The Way I Say It** • I will use effective word choice, voice, and sentence fluency. • My writing will be neat, and will have correct spelling, grammar, and punctuation.
Application: The Way I Connect to It • My story will be about something I know about.	**Application: The Way I Connect to It** • I will use my background knowledge and will include connections in my writing. • The narrative will include an overall theme, lesson, or purpose.

Consider the success criteria generated by two different classes for writing a persuasive letter, on page 38. Again, it is clear how the different expectations the grades are reflected in the targets set by the teacher and students.

As students and teachers work collaboratively to establish success criteria, they will develop a richer, deeper understanding of the goals they can set for themselves to become stronger, more proficient writers.

Sample Success Criteria: Persuasive Letter	
Grade 2 Success Criteria	**Grade 6 Success Criteria**
Knowledge: What I Write • I will use the form of a letter (greeting/salutation, body, and closing). • I will tell the main idea, all of the important details, and an important conclusion.	**Knowledge: What I Write** • I will clearly state the problem, my opinion, and the solution (call to action). • I will include an introduction and a conclusion that summarize my main ideas. • I will use the form of a letter (formal business style).
Thinking: What I Say • I will support my main idea with details. • I will organize my ideas in an order that makes sense.	**Thinking: What I Say** • My ideas will be logical, reasonable, and organized in a sequence. • My evidence will be connected to my opinion.
Communication: The Way I Say It • I will use neat writing, complete sentences, and organized paragraphs. • I will use correct spelling, punctuation, and capitalization. • I will use descriptive words and voice.	**Communication: The Way I Say It** • I will use clear expression and logical organization. • I will use formal voice, style, and tone. • I will use correct conventions (spelling, grammar, and punctuation). • I will use appropriate word choice, sentence fluency, and paragraphing.
Application: The Way I Connect to It • I will use my personal experience and knowledge to support my main idea.	**Application: The Way I Connect to It** • My writing will include personal connections to the topic. • I will use information from my research to support my opinion. • I will demonstrate why this issue is important.

An Example of Using Modeled Writing to Set Success Criteria

The following samples demonstrate the power of using strong teacher modeling as a source for generating success criteria. In this case, the teacher worked with the students to develop an outline and generate a complete writing sample that demonstrated a high level of success. The teacher modeled the writing process and the thinking processes associated with it. As she was writing, she engaged the students with rich dialogue about the word choice, sentence fluency, and voice of the piece. There were also discussions about the various elements of the piece (characters, setting, plot development, etc.), and how to effectively integrate them into the writing.

WRITING PROMPT: *Write an animal legend that tells how an animal got its unique features.*

How the Porcupine Got Its Quills
(Modeled Writing)

A long time ago, when the land was very young, there lived the porcupine. Porcupine was very lazy and irresponsible. His colorful soft fur was the envy of all the forest creatures. The other animals were jealous of his sleek coat, but disliked him because of his sluggish nature.

One late summer day, Bear gathered the animals and began to assign roles in order to prepare for the oncoming winter. All of the animals lined up eagerly, except for Porcupine, who had fallen asleep under the shade of a blackberry bush. Fox's keen ears heard Porcupine's loud snores. Fox followed the sound and discovered lazy porcupine fast asleep. Fox grasped Porcupine by his long soft tail and dragged him to stand before Bear.

Bear stood tall, and sized up the lazy Porcupine. Bear had spent all day assigning roles to the various forest creatures. With a snarl, he gruffly told Porcupine to gather berries and return promptly to the meeting place the following day.

Porcupine sulked away in search of fresh berries. No sooner had he found a heavily laden bush that his stomach started to growl. Unable to resist the temptation, Porcupine ravenously gobbled each and every berry in sight, completely covering his fur in a sticky black juice. After Porcupine's gluttonous feast, he fell fast asleep and forgot his responsibility.

Early the following morning, Bear summoned the animals for the meeting. Bear's loud roar abruptly awoke the slumbering Porcupine. In his fright, he scampered into the frail branches of the nearest poplar tree.

Bear's incredible sense of smell led him to the poplar tree in hopes of finding Porcupine's hidden supply of berries. Instead, he found a cowering Porcupine covered in blackberry juice.

Bear called to the Porcupine to come out of the tree, but he refused. Then Bear discovered that Porcupine had no berries to contribute. Bear was furious and in his anger shook the tree. Porcupine fell from the branches into a small, sharp pine bush below.

Porcupine struggled to get up. Because of the sticky juice, many of the pine needles had become firmly glued to his once-soft fur.

To this day, all porcupines are covered with sharp needles to constantly remind them of their need to contribute to the animal society.

From this modeled piece, the students generated the following success criteria:

Success Criteria for an Animal Legend

Knowledge
• I will demonstrate a good understanding of the parts of a legend.
• I will have a good story line and exciting plot development.
• I will include the elements of a narrative (setting, characters, plot).

Thinking
• I will include descriptive writing.
• My ideas will be logical and make sense.
• My writing will include lots of information to make the story fit together.
• I will have creative, detailed ideas.

Communication
• I will have correct spelling, grammar, and punctuation.
• I will think about my voice, word choice, and sentence fluency.
• My ideas will be organized into paragraphs.

Application
• I will include real characteristics of real animals.
• My legend will teach a lesson, have a moral, or support an overall theme.
• I will include connections to other animals.

In the two sample animal legends from the students in the class, it is interesting to note the similarities in the high level of word choice and descriptive writing. The students were able to apply many of the strategies demonstrated with a high degree of success, and it is clear that they were able to integrate most of the success criteria into their work.

How the Beaver Got its Flat Tail
by Marissa

One day a long time ago, by a pond like any other, lived Beaver. Beaver was very competitive and had never lost a competition. Beaver had yellowish buck teeth, soft blackish fur, brown beady eyes and a fuzzy, bushy, long tail.

It was summer and like most summer days was a calm, fine and peaceful day. Beaver and his friend were getting ready for their annual "who can build the best dam" contest. The contest rules required them to build the best possible dam in one day. When Beaver was finished practicing for the contest, he set off to see Wise Wolf for some high-quality advice.

When Beaver got to Wise Wolf's house Beaver was amazed to see him lying on the floor groaning! Beaver asked him what was wrong, and was expecting to hear a gigantic explanation about what had happened, instead Wise Wolf quietly whispered, "I'm sick."

"Will you be able to come to the contest tomorrow?" Beaver asked worriedly.

"No," Wise Wolf replied, " but remember that slow and steady wins the race and that I will always be in your heart cheering for you. Now Beaver, you must leave so I can get some sleep."

"Bye Wise Wolf," Beaver whispered.

On Beaver's trip home Beaver shrugged his head and thought that Wise Wolf's advice was useless. There was no way that he could win the race if he were to listen to him.

It was the day of the contest. Animals all over the forest were sitting around to get a first-class view of the contest. Beaver and his friend were both given a spot near the pond with five sharp sky-scraping trees.

Cheerful Chipmunk swung the flag and the competition began!

Beaver was chopping down trees carelessly and rapidly. He was on his last tree, but his competitor had already started to build his dam. With a careless rage to win, Beaver instantly started biting at the huge tree. Sadly, Beaver didn't notice the razor sharp branch. Beaver bit down firmly on the trunk and the loose branch fell off onto Beaver's tail. Beaver screeched with pain. Everyone rushed over to see what had happened to poor Beaver. Big Bear came over and lifted the branch off Beaver's tail. They all gasped. Beaver's tail had been not only flattened but all of the beautiful fuzzy fur on his tail had been skinned off.

After that devastating event, Beaver learned the importance of taking his time and paying attention to what he is doing. The words of the Wise Wolf echoed in his head, "slow and steady wins the race."

From this day on, beavers all over the world have flat hairless tails because of the one mistake that Beaver made.

The Skunk: Good Smell Gone Bad
By Scott

Long, long ago in the exquisite land of Canada, there was a majestic river with a vivid flow of clean water running like an eel swimming through a glittering lake. Everyday, a black cat with a white stripe bathed in the marvelous river. Black Cat adored her gorgeous fur and bragged about it often. "Look at my stunning fur! It's so shiny, soft and clean!"

"Yes, I know, you told me that already…" Beaver replied in an annoyed voice.

When Black Cat left to brag to someone else, Beaver thought of a plan that would make Black Cat stop bragging, with the help of a friend…

The next day, Black Cat was strolling on the side of the river after a nice, relaxing bath… and suddenly… the water started to shrink, and shrink, and shrink, until there was nothing left. "NO!" Black Cat shrieked and fainted. Black Cat didn't know that about two kilometers upstream, Beaver and his friends were building a dam.

Black Cat suddenly noticed a spirit three meters away. It looked like a blue-green gas. Vapor, maybe. It spoke to her in a deep, deep voice. "I am the almighty God of Happiness. I gave you the river because I enjoy love, but your egotistical nature made me deny and deprive you of it."

"No! No! You can't do this to me! NO!" Black Cat argued.

"You have no other choice. Also, you don't deserve the name Black Cat, you will now own the name… Skunk. " The spirit vanished.

"NO! NO! NO! NO! NO!" Skunk fell to the ground and cried.

After years of rotting, Skunk smelled terrible. Whenever she took a sniff, it reminded her of her terrible life, everybody ran away from her, so she had no friends or family. She was ashamed of herself. That was how the Skunk got its smell.

CHAPTER 4   *The Writing Process*

As students move from establishing success criteria to drafting their writing, there are many different areas that may serve as foci for instruction. While it is impossible to focus on everything at once, it is up to the teacher to incorporate a balance of form and content. The students need to develop an awareness of the elements contained in the specific form of writing they are learning, and ways in which they can develop the content to be meaningful and engaging for the audience. They might incorporate the traits of writing or find ways of thinking like readers, using different reading strategies in their writing. The number of areas that writers can focus on is somewhat overwhelming, so it is the art of teaching that helps us to know which skills need developing, and when. Once students have spent some time with the various skills and strategies, they will begin to seamlessly integrate the different skills into their writing. They will naturally flow between thinking of the elements of the text to ways of enriching their word choice, voice, or other writing trait; they will begin to think as readers as they write, considering the way the audience will connect with their words and providing tools for the readers to do so.

Writing With the Success Criteria in Mind

Youngsters are eager to try new tasks when they are sure of the desired result, as well as confident that their risk-taking will be respected and rewarded.

Having used exemplars, mentor texts, or modeled writing to co-construct the success criteria, students are now ready to write on their own. They have a very clear vision of the final product and a good understanding of the components that need to go into it to make it successful. They have observed the teacher working through the process of writing and watched as a final product demonstrates the success criteria. They have a good understanding of the final product, the success criteria that need to be included, and the process they can use to produce the desired piece of writing.

During this writing stage, it is important that the list of co-constructed success criteria is placed in a location that all students can clearly see, or printed as a handout for all students to refer to. Also, the writing modeled by the teacher should serve as a constant mentor piece for students to refer to during their own writing process.

One of the factors in developing strong writers is ensuring that students are engaged in the writing task. It is important that they have choice about their writing topic and feel that their writing is authentic and purposeful. This is a good time to revisit the four influences mentioned on page 16. In order to maximize student engagement, writing tasks need to take into consideration opportunities for students to meet all four of these driving forces: Accessibility, Authenticity, Audience, and Assessment.

- Accessibility: Providing students with adequate opportunities to organize their ideas, brainstorm new thoughts, or collect background information is important to the writing process. Nothing is more intimidating than staring at a blank page looking for inspiration. As teachers, we need to provide a range of writing opportunities for youngsters that appeal to their personal interests, and allow them to use their own experiences as a basis for their writing. We need to ensure that all students have access to the tools and strategies with which they are most comfortable.
- Authenticity: Students need to write about things that matter to them and are authentic to them. They need to write about things that excite them and fill them with wonder. Although the teacher has set the form or purpose for the writing, students should have the freedom to write about subject matter that they are personally connected to.
- Audience: Students need to think about the audience for their work and consider the way the reader will relate to the text. This is important so youngsters see their writing as valuable and real.
- Assessment: Finally, students need to have a clear vision of the desired target for learning and the success criteria for the task. They need to be actively involved in creating the assessment tools and have a thorough understanding of how their work will be assessed.

When writers are engaged and enthusiastic about the subject matter, perceive their writing as valuable and authentic, understand their audience, and are involved in the assessment process, they will be eager to fill the page with their thoughts.

As students begin to write, the role of the teacher changes from model to mentor. We move from demonstrating the writing to supporting the students as they try it out. Students have developed an awareness of the craft of writing, the product, and the success criteria. They are ready to apply this learning to their own work. It is possible for students to create a written piece either independently or cooperatively. There are benefits to both options, and teachers may wish to provide students with a variety of ways to try out new text forms. Older students especially enjoy the variety that comes with different learning experiences.

Shared Writing

When we invite students to join us in creating a piece of writing, they are actively participating in the process of creating a text. The piece of writing that is constructed through shared writing will help students understand the process of creating a unified piece of writing. Students need to feel that they are a part of the process, contributing their ideas and helping to form the writing that is being written by the teacher. However, the teacher has the ultimate control over the piece of writing. While constructing a piece together, it is important for you to remember that students will rely on this experience as a basis for their own writing. It is the beacon that will guide them toward a better understanding of the piece of writing they will construct independently. It should appear to our students as if they are directly affecting the outcome of the piece with their input, and they are; however, the teacher needs to have a firm vision for the direction the piece will go, and guide the students to this common understanding.

Cooperative Writing

When students are experimenting with a new text form, it is often helpful for them to write with their peers. Having someone to share ideas with while experimenting with new writing strategies will help students to deepen their understanding of the text form. It is beneficial for students to have the opportunity to articulate their thinking and learning to their peers, as well as to gain additional insight from the ideas of their friends.

According to Michael Fullen (2002), "information only becomes knowledge through a social process." In this light, when you invite students to actively engage with each other through social interactions, you will strengthen their understanding around the writing form. Students love making space in the room with a partner, a large sheet of chart paper, and markers in hand to work on a piece of writing together. Students of all ages enjoy these shared learning experiences. As we observe the students, we notice that they are experimenting with the writing craft and the various success criteria. Students are learning how to integrate the various features of the text style and the different writing traits. As they work cooperatively, they are able to keep the success criteria in mind as they strive toward the target.

Independent Writing

When students are ready to try out a new text form, teachers may opt to have them complete their first written piece independently. This gives students the opportunity to rely on their own experiences and strengths as authors to create their writing. It also gives them total creative freedom to write a piece that they would like to develop. This provides us with the opportunity to examine each student's strengths and challenges as they begin to transfer their learning to their own writing. When students write independently, we are better able to identify their individual needs and provide support for them. It is important that, as students begin to write, they remain aware of the success criteria that were constructed and strive to demonstrate them through their work.

Differentiating Writing Tasks

As we reflect on the four influences on writers, we need to ensure that we are providing adequate accessibility options for all students. Considering the different learning styles and interests within a group of students, we need to be always mindful of the different skill sets and prior experiences that students bring to their learning. Teachers need to give thought to providing students with a range of opportunities with which they can demonstrate their learning. Some students might feel more comfortable working independently; some might need to have social supports around them to share their thoughts with and work through their ideas. Some might be comfortable using computers to write, while others might choose to sit in a quiet corner with a clipboard. Regardless of the format that the writing may take, teachers need to recognize that different methods work for different students, and we need to provide adequate opportunity for students to explore and discover what works best for them.

What We Write

The different foci for instruction can be divided into two separate although connected areas: the form and the content. In other words, we need to look at what we write (the form), and the way we write it (content and style).

As students explore various forms of writing, they may notice that the greatest difference between forms occurs in the Knowledge area of learning. This indicates that good writing is good writing regardless of the form. In order to be an effective writer, one must include solid ideas (Thinking), clear Communication, and connections between the writing and one's knowledge of the world (Application). The Knowledge area of learning will differ across the different forms of writing, as students develop their understanding of what makes each form most effective.

As students move through the writing process from prewriting to drafting, we need to be aware of the skills and strategies that we are presenting to students through these stages. Through the exploration of sample texts (exemplars, mentor texts, or modeled writing), students and teachers are able to identify the important areas for focus. These will differ as the students move from one writing task to the next, and the teacher needs to intentionally build on the students' skill sets. As we continue to instruct students, their repertoire of skills will expand and they will be more able to apply them to their writing.

Knowledge

Beginning with a specific text form, students can explore sample texts that emulate the important features of that form to be able to identify the essential features in a complete piece of writing. Students are able to read and discuss sample texts and identify the necessary elements, defining them as success criteria for their own writing. As students recognize and define the various elements of each text form, these success criteria would typically fit under the Knowledge area of learning. Knowledge refers to the students' understanding of the form of writing: as they discover that all narratives, for instance, contain a plot, this would form the basis for the success criteria. The students might record this in their success criteria under *Knowledge*: "My narrative will contain a plot that includes a beginning, problem, and solution." The students have clearly identified a feature of the text form, defined it, and established it as a target for their own writing. Similarly, the students can explore a range of persuasive exemplars and determine that an effective text includes a convincing argument. They might include this in their success criteria, stating, "My persuasive writing will clearly state the problem, my opinion, and a convincing solution."

Thinking

As students explore the various sample texts, they may notice that the different forms have various features pertaining to the ideas contained in the text. For example, as students work to define the features of a procedure, they might notice that the steps are written in a logical sequence. In order to do this, the students must organize their ideas in a manner that makes sense. This would fit into the Thinking area of learning. They may include this as success criteria under *Thinking*: "My procedure will include ideas that are organized in a logical sequence."

Communication

Students will also notice that each text form has a different feel or voice. This concept will include some of these features under the area of Communication. Although most text forms will have similar strengths when it comes to Communication (sentence fluency, conventions, etc.), the success criteria may differ slightly, indicating small variances among the forms.

Application

Finally, the information contained in each form may vary as the students use their prior experiences, knowledge, and ideas to connect to their writing. Again, most text forms may reflect similar success criteria in the Application area of learning, as students are effectively finding ways of forming connections through their writing.

Although success criteria need to be balanced between the four areas of learning, teachers may select an instructional focus for each writing task. This may be a focus on the text form, or the content and style of the writing. Although it is important that students develop a holistic understanding of the skills associated with writing (balancing all four areas of learning), it becomes important not to introduce many new concepts at once. When students are familiarizing themselves with the use of success criteria, begin with skills that are familiar; gradually build on their skills, adding new targets as instructional foci for each subsequent writing task. As the year progresses, you will continue to build on the students' skills. For example, as students become more and more acquainted with the six traits of writing (see page 61), they will integrate this learning into their set of skills and use their knowledge of these writing strategies to refine the success criteria.

When we think of the form of writing, we think of the structure, the elements and style with which it is usually written. For example, when writing a narrative, we know that it must contain a setting, a plot, and characters; we also know that the plot needs to have a beginning, a problem, and a solution. This structure is what identifies a piece of writing as following a specific form. It is a framework for ideas to be organized upon. A narrative, by definition, includes these elements, and any deviation from these elements would make the writing no longer fit under the umbrella of that text form. When teaching students about new forms of writing, it is important that we help students develop an understanding of the specific elements that each form possesses. When we are using sample texts (whether exemplars, mentor texts, or modeled writing), it is helpful if we identify and label each feature. This will support students in developing an understanding that different text forms have specific features, and support them in being able to identify and include them in their own writing.

There are numerous purposes for writing, and each purpose has different genres, forms, and formats associated with it. Students might write to describe something, recount an event, or entertain their friends. They can write to express their point of view, organize their ideas, or share important information with others. Regardless of the purpose of writing, students need to become proficient at determining which form is needed in each situation and adjusting their writing accordingly.

- Genre: Within each text form, there are a wide range of genres. For example, a narrative is a text form, in that all narratives contain specific elements (setting, characters, and a plot); however, the possible genres of narrative are extensive. For example, a fairytale is a narrative, but so is a science fiction story, a realistic story, or a fantasy about dragons.
- Format: When considering the purpose and audience for each piece of writing, we see how the format of each text form can vary. For example, a procedural piece might vary in format when written for different purposes. A recipe would have a very different feel from the installation

manual for a new appliance; a persuasive piece will appear different if written as a letter or as an editorial article in a newspaper.

The possibilities for the variations of text forms, genres, and formats are almost limitless, so we will refer to the following text forms, into which most genres and formats of writing tend to fit: Narrative, Report, Recount, Procedure, and Persuasive Writing. When students develop an awareness of the different text forms and the strategies associated with creating them, they will become more adept at applying these tools to all writing occasions.

Narrative Writing

Narrative writing is writing that tells a story. It consists of a plot, characters, and a setting. Writers need to sequence their ideas in a logical way, so that the reader can understand how the various elements of the story are connected. The plot needs to include some form of conflict and a resolution. This is an important form in which students need to think about their voice, ideas, word choice, and sentence fluency. These traits, when combined with the features of a narrative, help to build fluent engaging stories.

Success Criteria for Narrative Writing

Success criteria that the students might identify when deconstructing narratives and setting success criteria for their own work include, but are not limited to the following:

Knowledge
- I will think about the topic, purpose, and audience for my writing.
- My writing will include the elements of a narrative (setting, characters, and plot; with a beginning, middle, and end).
- I will create an effective story line with creative/exciting plot development

Thinking
- I will develop my ideas in a logical and sequential way.
- I will organize my ideas so the story flows clearly.
- My writing will create visual images for the reader.
- I will include enough information to make the story fit together.
- I will include descriptive words and phrases in my writing.

Communication
- I will use my voice and word choice to enhance my ideas.
- I will use conventional spelling, grammar, punctuation, and paragraphing.
- I will use quotation marks for direct speech.

Application
- My writing will include some of my background knowledge.
- I will demonstrate my personal connections to my writing.
- My writing will include an overall theme, moral, lesson, or purpose to the story.

Narrative Writing Advance Organizer

Once the students and teacher have identified the success criteria for a given piece of writing, the students will need to begin planning and organizing their

See page 50 for the Narrative Writing Advance Organizer.

writing. As the students begin to think about their writing, they may find it helpful to use an advance organizer as a way of planning and recording their ideas. Using a graphic organizer allows young writers a format to think about their writing, and how their ideas will unfold in their piece. The Narrative Writing Advance Organizer on page 50 can serve as a helpful guide for students to begin to organize their ideas about their writing. They can use the various boxes to record information about the characters, setting, and plot. They might choose to think of ways to build suspense through the plot development, and enrich the readers' understanding of the characters through their different attributes. They can include descriptive words to help the reader envision the setting and understand the intricate components of the various characters' personalities. Writers might choose to record key words and phrases that may be helpful when drafting the first piece of writing.

Teacher Prompts

As students move from determining success criteria to drafting their writing, the teacher needs to continue to support the students in crafting their ideas. Throughout this time, use guiding questions to refocus the students' attention to the success criteria while they generate ideas for their own writing. While guiding students' thinking around this text form, the following prompts may be helpful to teachers in order to scaffold students' thinking and writing:

- What is your writing about?
- Why are you writing?
- What will be the problem/conflict in the story? How will it get resolved?
- For whom are you writing?
- How will you capture your reader's attention at the beginning?
- How might you create suspense/humor/foreshadowing/joy/empathy through your writing?
- What similar words or phrases could you use instead of _____ ?
- What time order words (*first, then, after, finally,* etc.) might help clarify the sequence of events in the story?
- Are there words or sentences in your story that make the reader understand how you (or the characters) are feeling?
- How can you help your reader make a picture of this in their mind?
- How do the sentences sound when you read them aloud?

Example of the Narrative Writing Process

WRITING PROMPT: *Students were given the phrase "He/She felt the little box in his/her pocket and smiled" and needed to include this phrase somewhere in their writing.*

The following short narrative is highly effective in conveying a strong emotion in the reader. This youngster was able to use strong word choice and vivid imagery to support her ideas. The overall mood of the writing is clear.

The Little Box
By Victoria

"Where am I?" asked Daniel in confusion.

"You're in the hospital." Replied his wife Taylor sweetly. Daniel remembered just a few days before when the nurses told him that he had pancreatic cancer.

Daniel knew that in only a few days time it would be Taylor's birthday. He had bought her a beautiful diamond necklace. His thoughts were interrupted by Taylor's voice.

"I'd better get going," said Taylor with a sigh. "I'll be back soon."

Just then the nurse came in to take him to the operating room. A little while later, Taylor returned.

"How'd it go?" Taylor asked the nurse eagerly.

"Not so well." Replied the nurse filled with regret.

As Taylor entered the room, there in the bed was Daniel with his hand outstretched. As she got closer she saw a little box in his hand. On it were the golden letters 'Happy Birthday'. She scanned his body frantically, hoping to see any sign of movement, but there was nothing. As she opened the little box, she found a beautiful diamond necklace.

A few days later, at Daniel's funeral, as the minister was speaking, she felt the little box in her pocket and smiled as the tears ran down her cheeks.

Narrative Writing Advance Organizer

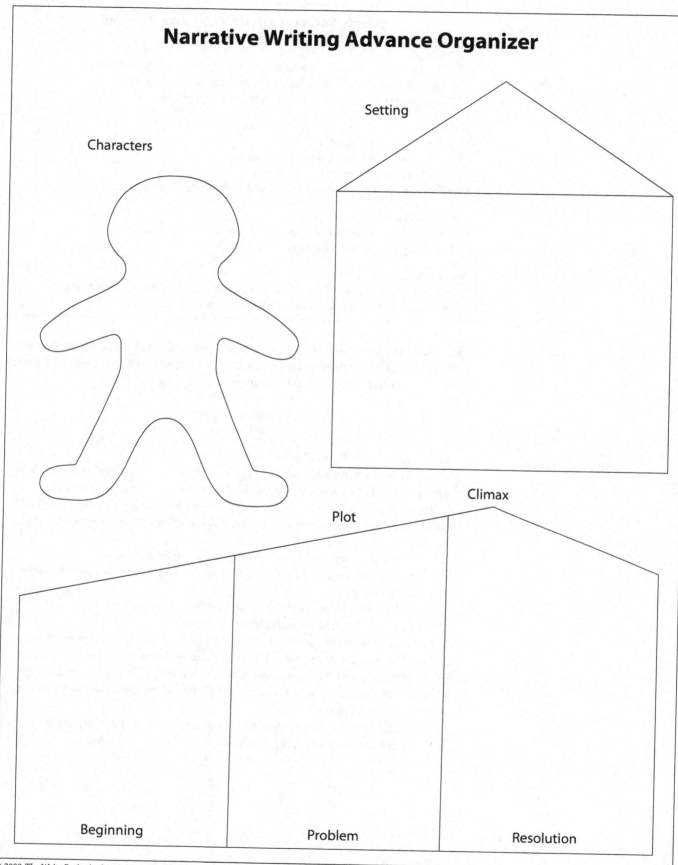

Characters

Setting

Plot

Climax

Beginning

Problem

Resolution

Report Writing

A report is a nonfiction, informational piece of writing includes facts. Students collect and organize information, and present it to the reader in a way of sharing important and interesting facts with others. Writers present facts in an unbiased manner and include few opinions and personal connections. Instead of including personal connections, students are invited to include evidence from various sources and find ways of connecting this information to present the whole picture of the subject being written about.

Success Criteria: Report Writing

Some skills students may need to think about include, but are not limited to, the following:

Knowledge
- I will remember to include an introduction and a conclusion that summarize my main point.
- I will include information that will provide a clear understanding of the topic.
- I will think about *Who? What? When? Where? Why?* and *How?* to help me gather and organize the information.

Thinking
- I will include interesting content and sufficient supporting details.
- I will organize information so that ideas are presented in a logical sequential manner.
- I will demonstrate a clear purpose and focus for my writing.

Communication
- I can use varying sentence structure and combining words.
- I will use vocabulary that is appropriate for the subject.
- I will use descriptive words, phrases, and ideas.
- I will use conventional spelling, grammar, and punctuation.
- I will organize my ideas into paragraphs.
- I will select the presentation style that would best suit the writing (print, graphics, layout, pictures, captions, etc).

Application
- I will use information from a variety of sources.
- I will evaluate which information is important and determine if it is suitable to include in the writing. If it is not suitable, I will gather more information
- I will use my personal experiences and prior knowledge to gather, organize and present the information

---

Report Writing Advance Organizer

See page 53 for the Report Writing Advance Organizer.

The Report Writing Advance Organizer on page 53 can be helpful to students as they begin planning their writing. They can organize their information under specific subtopics (*Who? What? When? Where? Why? How?*) that will help them later strengthen the internal organization of the piece of writing. Students can include words, phrases, and sections of research that they can later revisit and reorganize into a clear well-focused text.

Teacher Prompts

While guiding our students' thinking around this text form, the following prompts may be helpful to teachers in order to scaffold students' thinking and writing:

- Where will you find information for your report?
- How will you organize your ideas?
- Can you group similar ideas together to make paragraphs? Can you organize the paragraphs so they flow in a logical sequence?
- Did you find enough information? Do you think you should include all of the information you found? What will you do if you think you should add more to your report?
- How do you plan on capturing your audience's attention at the beginning?
- What do you want the reader to continue thinking about after reading your report?
- Have you provided enough information to support your main idea?
- What similar words or phases could you use instead of _____?
- How could you make your sentences and ideas flow together smoothly?
- Which resources could you use to help you improve your work?
- How will you share your work with your classmates?

Example of Newspaper Report Writing

The following sample of student work was written as a fictional report. Students used a mentor text to determine the success criteria for a report.

Sample Success Criteria: Newspaper Report

Knowledge
- I will demonstrate a good understanding of the parts of a newspaper article.
- I will include information that describes who, where, when, why, what, and how the event occurred.
- I will include the most important ideas at the beginning of the article, and the smaller details toward the end.

Thinking
- The article will use descriptive writing and will be interesting for the reader.
- The article will use evidence to support the main ideas.
- The article will include relevant information and explain the event in a clear manner.

Communication
- I will use quotes correctly.
- My article will use correct spelling, grammar, and punctuation.
- The article will be well-organized and -presented.

Application
- The article will include ideas and evidence to support the main ideas.
- Everything in my article will be important for the reader and will be relevant to the event.

Report Writing Advance Organizer

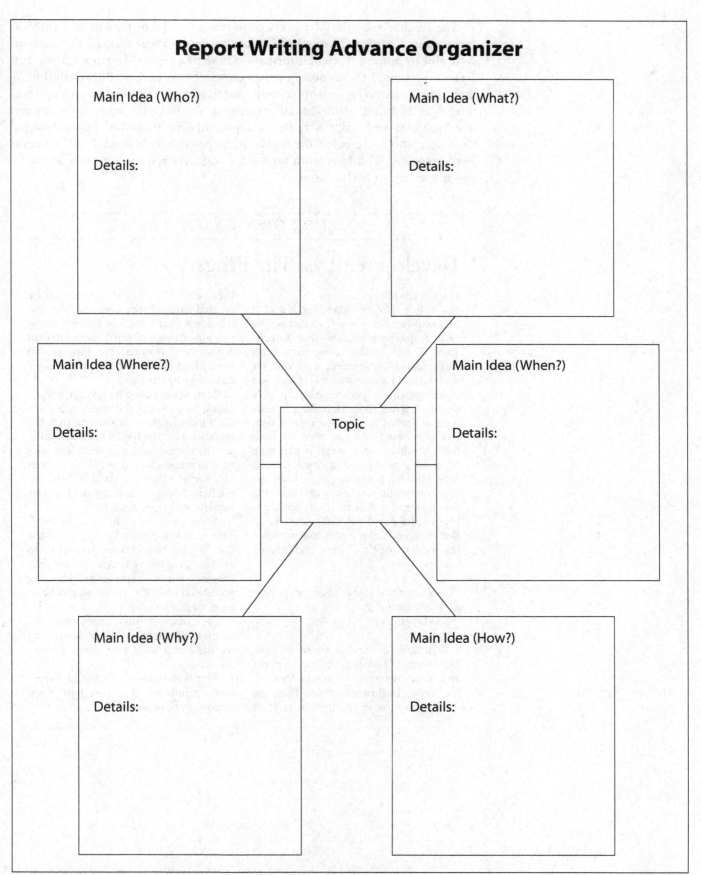

Main Idea (Who?)

Details:

Main Idea (What?)

Details:

Main Idea (Where?)

Details:

Main Idea (When?)

Details:

Topic

Main Idea (Why?)

Details:

Main Idea (How?)

Details:

The teacher role-played a press conference in which the students acted as newspaper reporters. Through this question-and-answer format, the students were able to gather sufficient information to write a report. The mock press conference presented the opposing perspectives of two parties: Bob DeBuilder, a high-powered developer who recently purchased a large area of land and was intending to build a substantial residential, commercial, and entertainment development; and Sally Mander, a representative from the Environmental Coalition who represented the highly endangered Green-Toed Toad. Students were presented with facts from both sides and were required to write a neutral newspaper report on the issue.

THE TOWN OBSERVER

Development vs. The Frogs

STAFF REPORTER: FIONA

Recently, on Wednesday March 25th a press conference was held to discuss the rare amphibian species—the Green-Toed Toad. At the conference, both DeBuilder Development Corporation and the Environmental Coalition expressed their perspectives on this sensitive issue. Bob DeBuilder, president of DeBuilder Development Corp. has purchased a large area of land for 42 million dollars and is planning to build a new housing development. Sally Mander, a representative from the Environmental Coalition says that the rare Green-Toed Toad is currently living on the proposed sight. She stated that this is one of the only four remaining habitats of this highly endangered species.

"I just want to do what's best for the people of the town."
- Bob DeBuilder

The area of land is slated to have low-income housing, schools, parks and two higher-end, luxury condominiums. DeBuilder insists that the development is in the best interest of the town, outlining the jobs that will be created through the construction and the opportunity for low-income housing for families affected by the recent economic downturn. "I just want to do what's best for the people of the town," he said sympathetically.

Mrs. Mander challenged the corporation to consider the need to protect the toads' habitat, explaining that the secretions on the toads' back may possess hidden secrets that may lead to a cure to meningitis, tuberculosis or even rare forms of cancer. At this time, the medicinal properties of the toad species remains only speculation.

"The toads can not be relocated," Sally stated emphatically. She explained that if the toads were relocated to another area where they could survive, the area would become quickly over populated and the species would be at even greater risk.

Ms. Mander was unavailable for further comment as her presence was required at a local tree-hugging ceremony.

The question remaining in everyone's mind is: "Are two legs more important than four?"

Recount Writing

A recount allows the writer to be reflective of an event or a process. Students present nonfiction information as it pertains to their personal experiences. Typically, a recount is presented in a sequential order, describing a series of events in the order that they happened.

Success Criteria: Recount Writing

Some skills that students will develop while writing include, but are not limited to, the following:

Knowledge
• I will describe an event or series of events in chronological order.
• My writing will be about a main idea and have a focused purpose.
• I will provide information about who, what, when, where, why, and how the event happened.

Thinking
• My recount will show how I have reflected on a personal experience.
• I will include details that describe how I felt and what I thought.
• I will describe the event using my five senses.

Communication
• My ideas will be written in a logical sequential order.
• I will include sequencing words to help organize my ideas (*first, then, finally*, etc.).
• I will use a voice and style in my writing that reflects my personality.
• I will use sentences that flow together.

Application
• My personal connections will be clear in my writing.
• I will clearly demonstrate my feelings through my writing.

Recount Writing Advance Organizer

See page 56 for the Recount Writing Advance Organizer.

The Recount Writing Advance Organizer on page 56 can be helpful to students when they are sequencing and organizing their ideas. They might choose to think of the big idea for the writing as a way of keeping the writing focused. Students then record words, phrases, and concepts that they plan on including in their writing. The sequencing words can serve as a guide for students, ensuring that their writing is presented in a logical smooth-flowing manner.

Teacher Prompts

Some prompts that can assist teachers in guiding their students' learning around this text form include

- What is most important for the reader to know about this event/process/thing?
- How do you feel about it?
- Can you include words that show your feelings?
- How can you use sequencing words (*first, then, finally*, etc.) to organize your ideas?
- What important lesson did you learn through this event?

Recount Writing Advance Organizer

Big Ideas:

First...

Then...

Finally...

- What do you want your reader to continue thinking about after reading your recount?
- Which parts can you describe vividly?
- How can you use your five senses to describe the event?
- How can you include feelings/emotions in your writing?
- How do you want the reader to feel after reading your writing?
- Which words can you include that will help the reader have a good mental image of the event you are describing?
- Which parts are the most important? Are there any parts that you could leave out and not alter the message you are sending to the reader?
- Are there any parts that you should describe more vividly than others?

Procedural Writing

This nonfiction form of writing is intended to let writers share the instructions for completing a task. In procedural writing, the most important traits to focus on are ideas and organization. Writers need to include sufficient details so their ideas are clearly understood by the reader, and their thoughts need to be organized in a logical sequential order so the reader can follow the procedure.

Success Criteria: Procedural Writing

Some skills that writers will need to think about include, but are not limited to, the following:

Knowledge
- I will include the materials and steps necessary to complete the procedure.
- My writing will clearly explain how to complete the procedure.

Thinking
- I will include steps that are necessary and relevant to completing the procedure effectively.
- Each step of the procedure will contain one main idea.
- I will present my ideas in a logical and sequential way.

Communication
- I will use sequencing words (or numbered steps) that will help the reader determine the order for completing the steps.
- I will use vocabulary that is specific to the procedure.
- I will write my directions with clarity and an appropriate voice.

Application
- My writing will demonstrate my personal experiences and prior knowledge with the subject matter.

Procedural Writing Advance Organizer

See page 58 for the Procedural Writing Advance Organizer.

The Procedural Writing Advance Organizer on page 58 can help students plan their writing. They can use the organizer to think about the steps involved in the process they are describing. They might also record any important things to remember—such as materials, essential steps in the process, or warnings that may need to be included.

Procedural Writing Advance Organizer

How To...

Important Steps:

Important Things
to Remember:

Teacher Prompts

The following prompts might be helpful when guiding students' thinking around procedural writing:

- Would someone be able to follow the steps in your procedure?
- Are the steps organized in a logical sequence?
- Have you included all of the materials and steps needed to complete the procedure?
- Which key words are important to include in your writing?
- Are there steps that require more detail than others?
- Is there anything that you think the reader may have trouble understanding (get confused with)?
- Do you need to include any sequencing words?

Persuasive Writing

This form of nonfiction writing shares the writer's point of view and is intended convince the reader to feel the same way. The writer needs to include sufficient evidence and details to support his/her opinion. The writer's voice and conviction is an essential element in this form of writing.

Success Criteria: Persuasive Writing

Some skills that writers need include, but are not limited to, the following:

Knowledge
- My writing will clearly express my opinion.
- I will clearly state the problem, my opinion, and a solution.
- I will include sufficient evidence/details to support the opinion.
- I will use an introduction and conclusion to present and summarize the issues.

Thinking
- I will use creative language to express a strong emotion.
- My ideas will be logical, reasonable, and organized in a sequence.
- My ideas will be connected to my opinion.
- I will support my ideas with details and reasons.

Communication
- I can use clear expression and logical organization.
- I will clearly present my opinion.
- I can demonstrate formal voice, style, and tone.
- I will use correct conventions (spelling, grammar, punctuation).
- My sentences will be fluent and I will use paragraphs to organize and present my ideas.

Application
- My writing will include personal connections to the topic.
- I will use information from other sources to support my opinion.
- I will demonstrate an understanding of why this issue is important.

Persuasive Writing Advance Organizer

Issue:

Opinion:

Main Idea #1

Supporting Evidence

Main Idea #2

Supporting Evidence

Main Idea #3

Supporting Evidence

Call to Action:

See the previous page for the Persuasive Writing Advance Organizer.

Persuasive Writing Advance Organizer

The Persuasive Writing Advance Organizer on the previous page can assist students with planning the information they will need to include to support their writing. They can use the various boxes to organize their information and evidence into main ideas. These main ideas can later form the basis for organizing the writing into paragraphs.

Teacher Prompts

Some prompts teachers may use to guide their students' thinking about this form of writing include

- What is your opinion on the subject?
- How will you convince others to agree with your point of view?
- How will you find evidence to support your opinion?
- How can you organize your ideas to best support your point of view?
- Which words will you use that will express how you feel about the issue?
- What do you want the reader to continue thinking about after reading your writing?
- What supporting details/evidence have you included for your point of view?
- Would this point of view be accepted by others? Why or why not?

The Way We Write It

If *what* we write comprises the specific features of the text form, then the way we write it reflects the content and the style with which we construct the piece.

Six Traits of Writing

Without a focus on voice, the writing may seem flat and boring; without a focus on sentence fluency, the writing may not flow smoothly and may seem choppy or rambling; without a focus on word choice, writing may seem simple and undeveloped; and without a focus on organization, the writing may seem disjointed.

In Ruth Culham's book *6+1 Traits of Writing*, she identifies six traits that strengthen student's writing: ideas, sentence fluency, organization, word choice, voice, and conventions. Sometimes presentation is considered an additional trait. By keeping these traits in mind, we are able to articulate the different strategies that writers apply in order to strengthen their message. Developing strong writers means much more than teaching students how to fit their ideas into a standardized template. A writer brings a wealth of personal style, voice, and experiences to writing that clearly defines it as good.

As our students establish an understanding of the different text forms, they also need to develop an awareness of the various traits of writing that help to give their work the style necessary to be engaging. These traits can be a focus for instruction regardless of the form of writing. Again, as we begin to balance the success criteria between the four areas of learning, we can introduce students to the different traits of writing through a wide range of writing tasks. As our writers write piece after piece, they are continuing to build their repertoire of skills, and we are continuing to add to their understanding of effective writing with each piece.

It would be overwhelming for a youngster to be faced with an extensive list of skills to include in their writing if they were not familiar with each skill on the list. We should not begin the year with all writing traits, but gradually introduce them to students through modeled writing, rich discussions of mentor texts,

This outline of the six writing traits includes guiding questions or prompts that teachers might find helpful when students are drafting their writing.

and identification through exemplars. You might choose to begin with one trait, such as word choice, and use this as a focus for instruction through modeled writing, then include it as a target on the success criteria for the writing piece. The next writing task might then have an additional writing trait, such as sentence fluency, as an instructional focus: the success criteria for that piece may include word choice and sentence fluency. In this way, you are gradually building the students' awareness of the traits of writing by integrating them into the different text forms. Once the students have been introduced to the different writing traits, they will discover that they are present in each form of writing—again, good writing is good writing regardless of the form.

Trait 1: Ideas

Ideas are the content of the writing, the theme of the message, and the details that support the author's ideas. When writers use interesting, unique, exciting ideas, it will make their writing much more appealing and engaging for all. Some questions that can guide students' ideas:

- What are you trying to say?
- What is the most important message that you want to get across to your reader?
- How can you select a focus for your writing?
- How can you make your message important, relevant, and engaging?
- What do you know about the topic?

Trait 2: Sentence Fluency

Sentence fluency is the way the words combine together to form sentences, and the way these sentences combine into smoothly flowing phrases and paragraphs. Sentence fluency is often described as the "auditory trait" of the writing, how we learn to read with our ears as well as our eyes. When writers effectively include sentence fluency, their work can be read aloud easily and is pleasing to the ear. Some questions that can help students focus on sentence fluency:

- How will you make your writing smooth and easy to read?
- How can you vary the sentence length and structure?
- How do your sentences sound when you read them aloud?
- Can you use the way the sentences work together to bring out your voice in the piece?
- How can you make sure that your sentences don't become too long or repetitive?

Trait 3: Organization

Organization is the way the author's ideas are combined into sentences and paragraphs. Organization needs to be logical, reasonable, and in an appropriate sequence. Various forms of writing require that specific elements be included and organized in a prescribed way. Some prompts teachers might find helpful to guide students' organization:

- How can you make sure that your message is clear in your writing?
- Can you make your ideas all support the main purpose of the piece?
- Which organizational format will be best suited to fit the purpose of your writing?

- How can you organize your writing so it will help the reader understand your ideas well?
- Can you include smooth transitions and connecting sentences and ideas?
- How will your beginning connect to your conclusion?

Trait 4: Word Choice

Word choice is the use of vivid descriptive language in the writing. It helps the reader to envision the words of the author and creates powerful images and emotions. It includes rich words and phrases that are new and exciting. The following prompts can help guide students' word choice:

- How can you make your writing clear and precise for the reader?
- Which words can you include to add depth, dimension, and description to your writing?
- Which sensory words could you use to help your reader visualize your words?

Trait 5: Voice

Voice is the reflection of the author's personality in his/her writing. It gives the reader a clear understanding of the author's intent. Voice is the way a writer conveys emotions and humor. It is the magic of turning words on a page into a story that comes alive in the minds of the reader. The following prompts can be helpful for students to develop their voice in writing:

- How can I recognize your personality through your writing?
- What does your reader learn about you through your writing?
- What does your writing sound like when you read it aloud?
- How can you convey strong emotions with your words?
- How will the reader feel after reading your work?
- Which voice would be best suited for the purpose of your writing?

Trait 6: Conventions

Conventions are the mechanics of writing. They are the communication elements that prepare the text for the reader. They are the standardized way of using spelling, grammar, punctuation, capitalization, and paragraphing. Some prompts that can support students with developing conventions in their writing:

- How can you make sure that you include correct spelling, grammar, and punctuation?
- Which resources can you use to support you when checking your spelling?
- How can you use conventions to make sure that your ideas are clear and your voice is expressed?

One More Trait

Presentation is sometimes included as an additional writing trait. Presentation is the way the writing looks on the page. When writers choose to produce a final piece of writing, they need to take into consideration the way it appears to the reader. This includes spacing and handwriting, use of titles, graphs, and illustrations as needed. Here are some teaching prompts that can be helpful when guiding students' thinking around presentation:

- How will you share your writing with others?

"The difference between the right word and the almost right word is the difference between lightning and a lightning bug."
— Mark Twain

- How can you make your writing appealing to others?
- Which form of presentation would best support your writing?
- How can you use titles, captions, illustrations, or diagrams to strengthen your writing?

Reading Strategies Become Writing Strategies

While writing this book, I began to think deeply about the four influences that are the driving forces for all writers (Accessibility, Authenticity, Audience, and Assessment). If writers are truly to think like readers, then they must also think of the reading strategies that the audience will use to connect to a text, and find ways to integrate them into their writing. As writers, we need to consider the audience and to provide the supports necessary for them to engage with the text in meaningful ways. If we want our readers to be able to visualize, then we must provide sufficient descriptive writing to support their thinking; if we want our readers to ask questions, then we must provide content that is thought-provoking and interesting.

As readers, students and teachers have become adept at identifying a range of reading strategies. We have become familiar with when and how to apply them. These include making connections, making inferences, asking questions, visualizing, determining importance, making predictions, and synthesizing. As readers, we engage in a dialogue with the text and, in so doing, have a conversation with the author. If we think of the connection between reading and writing, our young writers need to think of writing for an audience. They need to be aware that the words they write will be read by another person.

Writers need to think like readers, and remember that they are in control of the conversation that the reader will have with the text. Strengthening the reading–writing connection through reading strategies is an important link. As we are working with our youngsters, we need to pause and explain our thinking in relation to reading strategies. As writers, we need to remember that the text is a medium through which we communicate.

- In order to support the reading–writing connection, think about integrating some of the reading strategies into modeled writing as a way of building students' awareness of the way in which the audience will connect with the text. For example, when modeling writing, the teacher may use think-aloud: "I really want the reader to empathize with the main character, so I'm going to include some clues about how they are feeling."
- The reading–writing connection can be further strengthened in the drafting and revising process through thoughtful dialogue about the audience for the writing and the ways in which they will connect to it.

Visualizing

When readers visualize a text, they are creating a mental image of the concepts presented in the text. They are thinking about the sights, smells, sounds, and feelings that are conveyed through the writing. Authors need to provide sufficient details to assist the reader in forming these images. Prompts to encourage writers to think about providing readers with the opportunity to visualize include:

We need to assist students in carefully crafting their text in order to provide opportunities for readers to successfully apply reading strategies to their work.

Use the prompts or guiding questions when encouraging writers to think like readers and to find ways of incorporating the reading strategies into their writing.

- What words/phrases can you use that will help the reader picture/feel what is happening in your writing?
- How can you include enough description to give your reader a clear image of your ideas?
- What feelings do you think are important to include?
- How do you want the reader to feel after reading your work?
- What are you envisioning in your mind as the author?

Connecting

When readers make connections, they are forming personal links between the text and their own experiences. Authors need to include sufficient information and personal elements for the reader to connect meaningfully to the text. Prompts that can support student with providing their readers with connections include:

- How do you think the reader might feel about what you are describing?
- How do you want the reader to feel after reading your work?
- Which part do you think the reader may most easily connect with?
- How can you describe something so the reader can really understand what you are describing?
- What do you want the reader to know about you from reading your writing?

Inferring and Predicting

When readers make inferences, they are reading between the lines to draw conclusions. It is important for writers to provide sufficient information, but also allow opportunities for the readers to add their own thinking to the text. Through making inferences, readers determine the mood, theme, or feelings associated with the writing. When readers make predictions, they are engaging in a dialogue with the text by thinking about what could happen next. When writing, it is important to hold back some information, or include some elements of suspense, so the reader can fill in the gaps. Prompts that can support writers in providing opportunities for readers to make inferences and predictions include:

- What do you want the reader to conclude after reading your work?
- What is the theme, moral, or lesson that you want the reader to learn from your writing?
- How can you include some suspense or foreshadowing to give the reader some clues about what could happen next?
- How will the reader feel about your topic after reading your writing?
- Can you give your reader some clues about how to feel? How can you include words that convey emotions to the reader?

Determining Importance

When readers determine importance, they are figuring out the most important ideas in a piece of writing. They are able to think of the theme or big idea of the piece, as well as to identify the most important elements. As writers, we need to make sure that the piece of writing has a unified focus and the important information is clearly presented. Information must be presented so that the reader can easily identify the purpose and intention of the piece. Some prompts that can support writers in this area:

- What is the main idea of the piece of writing?
- What is the most important thing that you want the reader to remember?
- How will you make sure that the reader knows what the important message is?
- Which pieces of information are the most important? How will you make sure that the reader knows that these are important things to remember?
- Are there key words that you might use to draw the reader's attention to specific things in your writing?

Questioning

When readers ask questions, they are engaging in a dialogue with the text. They are posing questions and searching for answers. As writers, it is important to think about which elements in the writing may be confusing, and to provide sufficient clarification around those issues. Writers sometimes seize the opportunity of withholding specific information as a way of maintaining a reader's focus and attention. Also, writers may choose to include thoughtful questions in their writing in order to guide the readers' thinking. Some prompts that teachers might find helpful:

- What questions do you think the reader might still have after reading your work?
- Are there things that you want the reader to continue thinking about after reading your writing?
- How can you make your ideas clear for the reader? Do you think there are parts that may confuse someone? How can you make them better?
- Are there any thoughtful questions that you wish to pose in your writing?
- Do you think your writing will satisfy the readers' curiosity?
- How will you make sure that you don't leave any loose ends?

CHAPTER 5   *Conferencing and Coaching*

Effective Descriptive Feedback

In the next stage of the assessment-based writing process, students need to be provided with specific feedback as to their progress in terms of the success criteria. It is essential that feedback be effective and descriptive in order for students to embrace and apply it. Feedback that serves to motivate—such as "Great work!" or "I knew you could do it!"—might encourage learners, but it does not provide them with any guidance as to how they can improve their work. Feedback that is evaluative measures students' achievement with a score or grade. It can indicate to the student some level of their success, but fails to provide them with any direction for further learning. Feedback that is descriptive identifies students' areas of strength and provides them with specific guidance as to how they can move forward in the learning process. Feedback is most effective when students are encouraged to reflect on their work, recognize their strengths, and set goals for improvement.

Feedback is the vehicle through which we are able to guide students further along the learning process and closer to their goal. Students need to understand where they are in their learning and feel that they have enough input to set reasonable goals for themselves. Lorna Earle (2003) states, "It isn't enough for teachers to see the next steps and use them in their planning. Students need to see them as well." Although as teachers we recognize the importance of using assessment as a tool to guide our instruction, we are also aware that students need ongoing feedback about their individual progress. Students need support in establishing reasonable goals for their writing, and the most effective vehicle for strengthening goal-setting is descriptive feedback. In order for feedback to be an effective part of assessment, it needs to convey information to the student about where they are in relation to the success criteria, and to allow students to identify their next goals for further learning.

Effective feedback must contain information that a student will find useful and be able to apply. Earle (2003) demonstrates that feedback can lead to increased effort and engagement. She defines the role of the teacher as providing "signposts and directions along the way" that bring students closer to independence. Shirley Clarke (2001) encourages teachers to display the specific learning targets prominently in the classroom and revisit them frequently. In this way, we are able to ensure that they remain the fundamental focus for the learning.

Once students have had the opportunity to explore the sample texts, determine the success criteria, and draft a piece of writing, they are ready to begin to measure their progress. They continue to use the success criteria as a guide for their writing, reflecting frequently on the targets that were established at the beginning of the writing process. The teacher is able to provide feedback to

When we provide feedback to the students, we are providing students with an understanding of where they are in relation to the target. We are able to help them identify which success criteria they were able to demonstrate in their work, and which one would be the logical next step for them to continue to work on.

Using the success criteria is a way of keeping the target in mind throughout the learning process. As teachers, it is easy for us to become distracted by other influences in the classroom or in student's work; however, it is important that we remain focused on the specific learning intentions for each writing task.

"Effective feedback describes the student's work, comments on the process the student used to do the work, and makes specific suggestions for what to do next." — Susan Brookhart, "Feedback"

students that will help to measure their progress and set goals for the revision of the piece. Feedback needs to be specific to the writing piece and directly connected to the success criteria. The teacher can refer to the mentor texts as a way of guiding the student's revision process. Once some of the success criteria that the student was able to demonstrate successfully are identified, and one or two success criteria that are not yet being demonstrated (or could be strengthened) are found, the student has a very clear understanding of his/her current progress and the next steps along the writing journey.

When providing feedback to students, keep in mind previous goals. Student learning does not occur in isolated chunks; instead, each assignment continues to build the student's repertoire of skills. As students continue along this journey, we need to acknowledge their previous work and use it as a measure for their new learning. As students become more adept at setting goals, we need to ensure that adequate time is devoted to reflecting on these goals and measuring success in relation to them. We need to reflect on past writing assignments, encourage students to think about which personal goals they set for themselves, and help them recognize how they have attempted to apply that learning to their subsequent pieces of work.

According to Susan Brookhart (2008), the most effective feedback focuses on the qualities of the students' work, or the strategies and processes that they used to produce the work. When giving feedback to students, it is important that teachers know their students well and tailor the amount and type of feedback to best suit the needs of individual learners. Based on the work of Brookhart, these suggestions might help you provide students with feedback:

- Feedback needs to be timely. We need to provide students with feedback about their learning while the student is still thinking about the learning.
- Feedback needs to be purposeful. Feedback that is provided to students needs to be skill-specific, rather than task-specific. Provide students with feedback about things that they will continue to have an opportunity to practice.
- Limit the amount of feedback. Don't try to correct everything; instead provide feedback about the most important, relevant, and useful areas.
- Consider the most effective mode through which to deliver feedback: written or oral; if oral, individual or group.
- Relate the feedback to the goal. Describe students' learning in terms of the success criteria and assist them in setting goals that will move them closer to their target.
- Feedback should be free of judgment. Feedback should describe students' learning and assist them in setting targets, rather than being an assignment of a mark or judgment.
- Identify ways in which a student's work has improved and suggest one or two goals that are attainable for next time.
- Use a tone that demonstrates respect for students as being in control of their learning.
- Try to pose questions that cause the students to become reflective of their work in relation to the success criteria.

Ruth Culham (2003) defines *revision* as taking an idea and moving it along; whereas *editing* is the process of "getting things right." When we revise, we add details, reorganizing our ideas so that things fit together better or flow in a more logical sequence. We further develop our thinking so it becomes perfectly clear

We need to resist the urge to edit and correct a student's writing, remembering that they are ultimately in control of their learning.

to the reader. When we are editing, we are ensuring that the spelling, grammar, punctuation, and paragraphing are correct. We are fixing our writing to fit with the conventions of written language. Culham states that the writing traits of ideas, organization, voice, word choice, and sentence fluency are traits that students need to address during the revising process, whereas conventions and presentation are the areas of focus when editing. In this light, when providing feedback with students, we need to ensure that it enables students adequate opportunities to focus on both revising and editing strategies.

In short, feedback needs to provide evidence to the student about where they are in relation to the learning targets. Feedback needs to acknowledge and praise students' progress and growth. It needs to give students time to reflect on their learning and consider their next steps. Feedback needs to balance opportunities for revising and editing. We need to make sure that the feedback we are providing is specific to the needs of each student or the group of students with which we are conferencing. Feedback needs to provide students with clear, logical, attainable next steps in order to continue their learning. Finally, it is important to remember that feedback is a reciprocal process in which students are active participants and reflective learners.

Forms of Feedback

It is important to consider the different needs and learning styles of students and adjust the form of the feedback, as well as the content, to best suit the individual needs of each student. Feedback might look different in different classrooms, and even within one classroom. For example, a teacher might decide to provide written feedback to some students, conference with groups of learners, and meet individually with others—all to meet everyone's needs.

Feedback can take many different forms. As teachers, we need to think about which form will be most effective for our individual students. We might decide to provide feedback in written or oral form, through a structured writing conference or informal interaction between the teacher and student. No matter what mode is chosen for feedback, it is important that students receive clear concise messages about where they are, where they are going, and the next step they need to take to get there.

Time, as always, remains a factor to be taken into consideration. In order for feedback to be timely, the teacher needs to find effective strategies in order to touch base with each student while he/she is still thinking about the learning, focused on the task, and reflective of the process gone through to create it. Feedback needs to be focused on the learning target, be based on the success criteria, and provide guidance that will assist students in moving forward in their learning. As we examine the varying learning styles of students within one classroom, we need to find creative ways to ensure that all students are provided with meaningful feedback that they can understand and relate to.

Regardless of the form feedback takes, it is important to always identify the strengths of the student's writing, followed by one prompt that will help the student identify an area for improvement. It is helpful to think of these as "two stars and a wish": the two stars identify ways in which students were able to demonstrate the success criteria in their writing; the wish is a prompt that will help them reflect on their work and set a goal for themselves. It could look something like this:

The connections to your personal experiences are clear.
Your voice is strong and you have used descriptive words.
Many of your paragraphs start with similar phrases. How can you use different words to start each idea?

Written Feedback

Written feedback is helpful because it creates a record of each student's growth. When you write feedback in a student's notebook, it becomes easy to reflect on past writing assignments and consider the student's accomplishments. We are able to review past writing goals, set new ones, or revisit ones that remain areas for continued growth.

The biggest challenge with written feedback is ensuring that students read and understand the feedback that is given. Some teachers find it helpful to write the feedback on the top of the next page that the student is to write on. That way, the next time the student begins to write, he/she will take a moment to reflect on the feedback provided previously. Another way to ensure that students have read and understood the feedback is to encourage them to create a response; e.g., identifying a goal for the next piece of work. A third way is to encourage students to share their feedback with a friend. In this way, they are able to articulate the things that they did well and share an area upon which they plan to focus. Finally, you might find it effective to have a brief informal conversation with students about their feedback, asking them to identify their strengths and a goal for themselves.

Oral Feedback

The biggest advantage of oral feedback is that it provides opportunities for the student and teacher to have a dialogue about a given piece of writing. As we know, learning is a social process; students need to be able to articulate their thinking in order to process it at a deeper level. Engaging with students in a dialogue about their writing provides them the opportunity to share their intent, purpose, and goals for the piece of writing. Taking the time to listen to young writers provides us with much greater insight into their learning than just reading the words they have written. As we conference with students, we may become more aware of things they are experimenting with as writers that we may have missed had they not had the opportunity to share it with us.

Conferencing with students orally provides them an opportunity to share their successes and challenges as writers and to draw our attention to specific features in their work. Providing feedback orally gives us the opportunity to redirect students' learning and correct any misunderstandings that may have occurred. These short interactions between teacher and student allow for mini-lessons and review as it pertains to individual student needs. The time that we invest in providing oral feedback to students is well worth it. Students savor the small-group or individual attention, and are given specific guidance that will help them become stronger writers.

The biggest challenge with providing feedback orally is that teachers need to find a way of recording the information that is shared. Although engaging in a dialogue is highly effective for both learners and teachers, it is important that the essential ideas from the conference be recorded for review at a later date.

Informal Interactions

As we informally monitor our students, we are constantly providing feedback. When we observe students working, we are able to provide short bursts of feedback during the writing process that can help students keep focused on the goals

Anne Davies (2008) suggests using look-for-proof prompts that focus students on sharing specific skills that they would like us to attend to when providing feedback:

- This work shows how I've improved because…
- I'm starting to…
- I tried hard to…
- Please pay attention to…
- I've really been working on…
- I was experimenting with…
- I think I've improved on…
- I think I've reached my goal of…
- I am most pleased with this piece because…

"A critical part of teaching writing is having students talk about their writing before they write, while they are writing and even afterward. Scaffolded conversations with students are essential for producing excellent coherent texts." — Regie Routman, *Writing Essentials*

Regardless of the form of conference, it is imperative that the student remain in control of his/her writing at all times. During a conference, teachers need to resist the urge to pause midsentence to alter a grammatical error or inadvertently insert the correct spelling of an illegible word.

See the Success Criteria Checklist and Feedback form on page 89.

of their learning. We comment on their creative strategies and ideas; we provide gentle reminders about the success criteria and prompt students to consider how they can incorporate them into their writing. This informal feedback is very helpful for students as they are working through a piece of writing.

Formal Conferences

A writing conferences is very useful for providing effective descriptive feedback about a completed piece of writing. Students can conference with the teacher individually or in small groups.

Meeting with students individually allows for very direct specific feedback that is individually tailored to meet that student's needs. Individual conferences allow students to articulate their thinking, listen to the feedback, and ask questions they may have in order to clarify their understanding. It is important that conferences be brief and focused.

If we conference with students in small groups, we can organize learners together in order to reach a broader group of writers. In group conferences, students need adequate opportunities to share their individual successes and challenges. When we meet with a group of students, these students are able to serve as social supports for each other as they begin to reflect on the conversation that they had with us. They are then able to share their individual and collective goals, and provide a network of peer support as they continue to work toward those goals.

Conferencing is most effective when students meet with the teacher to measure their writing in terms of the success criteria co-constructed before the writing began. When the teacher and the student have a shared vision of what a successful piece of writing looks like, it becomes much easier to have a conversation about how close a particular student's current piece of writing is to meeting those targets.

When conferencing with students (individually or with a group), encourage students to share first what they feel they did well in their work in terms of the success criteria. Students should also reflect on their writing and think about one (or two) things that they need to continue working on or forgot to do. It is helpful if the success criteria are posted in a location that is visible for students during this discussion, or are distributed to them to refer to during their writing and conferencing. Sometimes students give specific examples from their work where they demonstrated a specific skill, and it's great to celebrate these successes together.

When providing feedback, use a similar pattern. Identify the student's strengths first by describing ways in which the student was able to apply the success criteria to the writing. Using evidence from the writing to support your discussion, share ways in which the writing is strong. By keeping the success criteria in mind, select one skill that the student should continue to work on, to improve his/her writing. It is important that the point for continued growth is one that the student has some familiarity with. This is not the time for introducing new learning. This is the time to encourage the student to become more reflective on the writing as a whole. Students need to change their thinking: instead of considering this a time when they can have their spelling and grammar corrected, they should see conferencing as a time when they are given the opportunity to rework a piece of writing, improve it, learn from it, and apply this to subsequent pieces of writing.

Once students become familiar with the process of conferencing for feedback, it becomes a natural transition for them to engage in peer conferencing. As students become comfortable with identifying their own strengths and setting goals, they are able to engage in these dialogues with their peers. This learning through social interaction is invaluable. As students are able to articulate their learning with others and reflect on the learning of others, they are internalizing the skills and strategies needed to become self-monitoring writers.

Focus for Feedback

"Perfectionism is the voice of the oppressor." —Anne Lamott, *Bird by Bird*

Although the process of giving feedback is important, the focus for feedback is equally important. When establishing success criteria with students, it is important that there is a balance between areas of learning: Knowledge, Thinking, Communication, and Application (see Chapter 3). In short, skills that are connected to Knowledge include an awareness of the form of writing and the necessary components. Thinking skills demonstrate a student's creativity and understanding of the way ideas can be best presented. Communication skills include the conventions of writing, as well as the style of writing (including voice and word choice). Finally, Application refers to the student's ability to form connections through writing and link ideas to previous experiences. Writing is a balance of all four areas.

As we provide feedback to students, we need to decide which area is the most important for their continued growth. We need to point out the successful features of the piece of writing, then narrow the focus for improvement to one or two attainable skills that the student can work on. In some cases, students might need to review the elements or text form; perhaps they have neglected to include an important feature or need to make their ideas clearer. Some students need support adding descriptive writing or organizing their ideas to flow smoothly together in a logical sequence. Some youngsters need to think about how they can introduce more of their own voice or personal experiences into their writing. And some young writers need to think about enriching their ideas with details and evidence. It is important for students to recognize that writing is the process of recording one's ideas so that others can read them. Writers need to be encouraged to take risks, use new and exciting words, and find their voice.

As we prepare feedback for our students, it is important to consider which skill is the most important area for continued growth and development, and draw the student's attention to it.

We all recognize the importance of using conventional spelling, grammar, and punctuation; however, it is important that providing feedback to students does not turn into an editing session. Conventions are only one part of one of the four areas of learning. Although it is important that students develop strong editing skills and use conventional spelling, grammar, and punctuation, it is equally important that students are encouraged to develop their ideas, find links to their personal experiences, and experiment with a range of text forms. We need to make sure that students do not sacrifice their word choice in an effort to have perfect spelling. It is much better that a child spell a word incorrectly and take a risk than that child settle for familiar, comfortable words. Too frequently, too much emphasis is placed on the mechanics of writing rather than the ideas and content therein. As an artist would not polish a sculpture until she had finished forming it by carving and refining it, likewise writers need to shape the writing pieces, focusing on the ideas and form, before polishing the spelling, grammar, and punctuation.

The importance of narrowing the focus of feedback to one specific area for growth was demonstrated by the students in a Grade 6 class, who were completing newspaper articles. One youngster was sulking about not wishing to share his work. When his friend looked at what he had completed in the time allotted, the friend gasped and exclaimed, "He hasn't done anything! He was supposed to have it complete and it's just a bunch of jot notes." The student was invited to have a writing conference and share his work thusfar. When the conference was concluded, he left with a renewed enthusiasm, returning to his desk to do just the "one" thing that he needed to do. You see, he was told the things he did well: he had lots of supporting evidence; he had identified the who, what, when, where, why, and how of the incident; his evidence was clearly connected to the main idea of his article. All he needed to do was write it into sentences and paragraphs. What initially had seemed like an overwhelming task now seemed minimal, because it was just one thing to work on and he was able to celebrate the successes he had already had. Just one thing—write it in sentences and paragraphs.

CHAPTER 6

Revising, Reworking, or Retrying

What Next?

Students have invested a great deal of time creating an understanding of the components of a piece of writing, they have observed a real writer at work, they have had the opportunity to try it out, and they have received valuable descriptive feedback. So now what? What do we do with this piece of writing that has been created?

Surely it is a starting point, although for the students it may feel more like an end point. Only once we have a chance to assess students' authentic writing are we able to assist them in setting goals for themselves. However, as is often true in a classroom, the thought of rewriting a piece is overwhelming. Youngsters who have struggled to compose a piece of writing might feel frustrated if, after every conference, they are presented with feedback that results in a back-to-the-drawing-board feeling. That is not the intent for feedback. Feedback is not intended to result in one perfect piece of writing; rather it is to shape the student's awareness of the process of writing. Each conference should build on the previous one and continue to build the student's awareness of what good writing is. It is, in essence, the writer we are shaping, rather than the writing. As teachers, we need to be sensitive to how our young writers are perceiving our feedback, and we need to encourage, guide, and not overwhelm. Thus the next step for each piece of writing is a crucial decision that needs to be made with caution.

We need to recognize that the writing–feedback–writing process is not linear, but rather is a reciprocal process whereby the feedback builds on the writing, and the writing is built on the feedback. However, students need to be provided the opportunity to apply the information gleaned through the feedback process. This application stage is important in order for students to begin to see direct connections between the feedback they receive and the way they can apply it to their own writing. Students may apply the feedback in one of three ways: revising, reworking, or retrying.

Revising

When students are asked to revise their work, they need to make adjustments to it that do not require them to recopy it. For very young writers, this is a great option for applying feedback. They do not need to spend their time copying their own words, and can simply find ways of revising parts of it in order to make it better. For example, in a primary grade, a youngster might need to insert a sentence or two to clarify an idea, add detail, or insert a feeling into a piece of writing. Older students might need to insert paragraphs, or delete and

Michelangelo said, "Every block of stone has a statue inside it and it is the task of the sculptor to discover it." As we assist in shaping young writers and their work, we must be mindful of which areas are the most important to focus on at various points in their learning.

rework sections of text; however, the whole piece does not need to be rewritten. With this simple quick fix, students are easily able to apply new learning to their writing and see immediate results.

Reworking

When students rework their writing, they need to rethink some sections of their writing in order to make it better as a whole. Reworking is a big task and may involve rewriting chunks or even the entire piece of work. This might include reorganizing ideas to flow together more smoothly, or clarifying their thoughts so the main purpose of the writing becomes clear. When reworking, students often find it easier to work with a computer, since it is easier to cut-and-paste sections of text and quickly reorganize or revise necessary sections.

Reworking is the most time-consuming process of the three options, and students need to recognize the improvement that the investment of time will make to their final draft. Reworking should not be confused with rewriting, in that the writing is evolving and being shaped by the author throughout the process. When reworking, the writer is finding ways of applying the feedback to the piece as a whole and reshaping it so it becomes a stronger piece of work.

Retrying

When retrying, students are given the opportunity to apply the feedback to a new piece of writing. Students write a new piece of work in the same form, genre, or style as a way of working toward their writing goal. In this way, students can use their learning from the feedback to develop another piece that is stronger and closer to their writing targets. With younger students, if the task remains similar to the previous one, they are more easily able to find ways to apply their learning to this new task. Older students might be able to apply their writing to a broader subject area; however, the form and genre of writing should remain the same. When retrying, students usually are eager to apply their new learning and relish the opportunity to use their creativity to create a new piece of work.

Example of Response to Descriptive Feedback

In the following writing sample, the effective power of descriptive feedback is clearly demonstrated.

WRITING PROMPT: *Write a letter to the principal convincing him/her to change something about the school that matters to you.*

Success Criteria for a Persuasive Letter

Knowledge
- I will clearly state the problem, my opinion, and the solution (call to action).
- I will use details/evidence to support my opinion.
- I will include an introduction and conclusion that will summarize my opinion.
- I will use the form of a letter (salutation, body, closing).

Thinking
- I will use creative language to express a strong emotion.
- My ideas will be logical, reasonable, and organized in a sequence.
- My ideas will be connected to my opinion.
- I will support my ideas with details and evidence.

Communication
- I will use clear expression and logical organization.
- I will demonstrate formal voice, style, and tone.
- I will have correct conventions (spelling, grammar, punctuation).
- I will demonstrate my word choice (descriptive words, action verbs, appropriate environmental vocabulary).
- My sentences will be fluent and I will use paragraphs.

Application
- My writing will include personal connections to the subject.
- I will use the information from my research to support my opinion.

Here is Jessica's first draft of her persuasive letter. This youngster wrote a first draft that contained many of her ideas, but lacked the organization, flow, and conventions to make it an effective piece of writing.

Dear Principal,

We would like to be able to listen to our I-Pods and MP3 players at school. We think listening to music daily will increase our imagination, focus and music is good for your mind.

We would like to be able to listen to our I-Pods and MP3 players during tests so the other people wont talk. Also people will be able to focus more and that way it will incurige us to finish faster! We would also like to throw out another point which is that if we focus more and don't talk it will take stress off other people.

We strongly recommend to listen to our I-Pods and MP3 players during Art so that our emagination is nicer and again so we can focus on our work that way our work will look better in a shorter time! And it will show our imagination.

Our ipods or MP3 players taking part or our daily life has been sentifically proven that it helps our brain and is good for your life.

if you alow us to listen to our ipods and MP3 players at school it will increase our imagination, focus and will be very good for our minds.

Sincerely,

Jessica

This student was given the following feedback:

- Your writing includes three main ideas in the opening paragraph and you have given some evidence for them throughout the piece.
- Your writing follows the form of a persuasive letter (including an introduction, three main ideas, and a call to action).
- You have somewhat organized the information into paragraphs and remembered to include a greeting, body, and closing for the letter.

Think about how you can provide evidence for each main idea as a way of building your ideas and making them clearer.

Also, how can your word choice help the reader understand how important this issue is to you?

Jessica chose to rework her letter, and ended up with the following final draft.

Dear Principal,

Some of our students think that we should be able to listen to our I-Pods and MP3 players at school. We think listening to music daily will increase our imagination, focus and music helps you stay alert.

We strongly recommend that you allow us to listen to our I-Pods and MP3 players during some subjects because our imagination and creativity will become stronger. Also, for some people music puts you in a good mood so that you will never be mad. If you are never mad, we think that it would reduce fights and disagreements. We also recommend listening to I-Pods and MP3 players using sweet or mellow music that way you can be relaxed and it will reduce distractions.

We would like to be able to listen to music during our independent time, that way it will diminish the amount of people talking. Also if we were to listen to our music, we could focus on our work and finish faster. We would also like to listen to music because it would help us to concentrate.

Our I-Pods and MP3 players taking part of our daily life will make us stay alert, which connects to everything else, helping us concentrate, imagine things and focus.

Sincerely,

Jessica

It is clear that this student was able to apply the feedback that she was given as a way of refining her writing. The second piece is a much more articulate, organized, and effective piece of writing.

When to Publish? What to Publish?

Publishing is the final stage of the writing process. It is the stage where writing is prepared for sharing with others. As important as the publishing stage is in the writing process, it is not possible, nor advisable, that every piece of writing make it to this stage. When publishing writing, the focus shifts from the process of writing to the product that writing produces.

All young writers need to have opportunities to share their work with others and select some pieces that they would like to polish. When selecting a piece to publish, students need to make sure that they have made it as conventionally correct as possible. This is the time to edit for spelling, grammar, and punctuation. Publishing a piece of work gives it authenticity and provides opportunities for students to celebrate their success as an author.

In one school, Kindergarten students proudly display their writing for all to admire, and under each is a caption that states the individual strength for each piece of work; e.g., "Sara is famous because she uses exciting words," "David is famous because he remembered to use a period," and "Matthew is famous because his sentences told a story." What an amazing opportunity for these young writers to share their work with the school, and what a brilliant teacher who took this opportunity to clearly identify the success criteria of this writing project! Even youngsters in Kindergarten are able to identify the components of good writing and find ways to apply them to their own work.

CHAPTER 7 *Assessment and Reflection*

Assessment and Evaluation

Assessment is the process through which we develop a deeper understanding of our students. It helps us evaluate the effectiveness of our teaching strategies and refine our approach as needed. For teachers, assessment is an essential component in any reflective teaching practice. It is through ongoing assessment that we are able to understand the impact that our instruction is having on student learning and to differentiate our strategies to better suit the needs of the various learners. However, the benefits of assessment are not one-sided. Students are also highly influenced by ongoing assessment. Through regular assessment and feedback, students are able to measure their success in terms of their learning targets and set realistic goals for their continued growth and development.

Throughout this book are references to the three guiding questions of assessment: Where are students going? Where they now? And how can they close the gap? These key questions form the basis of assessment *for* learning. Through the assessment-based writing process, students are able to articulate where they are going (in terms of the sample texts and success criteria), where they are now (in terms of their self-reflection on the success criteria and descriptive feedback), and how they can close the gap (determined through feedback and goal-setting). This reflective process of moving ahead while looking back assists students in becoming more aware of their skills, needs, and goals as writers. Involving students in the assessment process is critical to enabling them to become more accurate and effective in guiding their own learning.

Assessment should not come as a surprise at the end of a given assignment, instead it should be a clear standard that students are aware of, helped to create, and can use themselves to measure their success. When we use the student-constructed success criteria to guide the assessment tools, then the students are very aware—from the beginning of the writing process—of the skills that will be evaluated at the end of the process.

Through assessment, students are provided with feedback that is intended to focus their learning and guide their next steps. Assessment is about determining logical goals for students and teachers through an ongoing reflective process.

In contrast, evaluation is the process through which a student is assigned a mark, grade, or evaluation. This process is also important because, as teachers, we are responsible for reporting student learning in quantifiable terms. But, although evaluation is important in reporting student progress to others, it does not typically tend to directly affect student learning. The evaluative process serves to provide a snapshot to others about where each student is in relation to the learning expectations for a given grade, unit, or skill. Evaluation is synonymous with assessment *of* learning. It is a summative process that is completed

Often the terms "assessment" and "evaluation" are used interchangeably; however, they are different processes, with separate purposes and different outcomes.

As teachers, we need to recognize the differences between assessment and evaluation, between assessment *for* learning and assessment *of* learning. We need to use assessment to guide our instruction and assist students in setting goals, and we need to use evaluation processes to measure and report on student achievement.

During the process of writing this book, I shared the concept of student-constructed assessment tools with a fellow teacher. I was taken aback when he asked if there would be any "quantifiable" measures in the assessment tools, such as "having 22 words in a sentence." A statement like "22 words in a sentence" would not in any way serve to assess or develop young writers. When we are designing our assessment tools, we need to ensure that the targets we are assessing are firmly based in the guidelines provided through the curriculum.

We need to think of creating assessments as a way of discovering as much about a writer as possible.

after an event or learning, and is able to measure the student's achievement in terms of a standardized level of achievement.

When students are actively involved in the assessment and evaluation processes, they become more meaningfully engaged in their learning. Working with students to generate assessment tools, such as checklists and rubrics, we support them in measuring their learning in terms of the targets. When the students actively participate with the criteria used to assess their learning, the assessment will be more valuable to them. They will understand the components that are being assessed, the skills that are being considered, and the suggestions that are being made to further guide their learning.

What Should Assessment Be Based On?

Assessment needs to be firmly based in curriculum guidelines and assessment standards. As teachers, we need to be conscious of the expectations for each grade level and to plan our assessment tools with them in mind. The assessment tools need to be designed in a way so that they are clear to students and connected to the specific curriculum.

When we construct assessment tools, it is important that they reflect a range of areas for learning. The whole picture is made up of different parts, and it is important that these areas be balanced. Targets need to include skills that reflect the student's understanding of the text form and style of writing; they need to reflect students' ability to communicate their thoughts to others; they need to consider the way students make use of their personal connections and background knowledge; and, finally, they need to evaluate students' thinking and creativity when presenting their ideas. When we take the four areas of learning into consideration (Knowledge, Thinking, Communication and Application), we need to ensure that the targets span these different areas. Although teachers and students are constructing the assessment tools, we are not re-inventing the important elements that need to be assessed through the students' work. For assessment to be valid and purposeful, it needs to assess the specific curriculum guidelines for each grade. Teachers are encouraged to use the curriculum as a guide for developing assessment tools with the students.

As instructors, we need to remain vigilant of the skills that we need to teach and assess, and ensure that these are introduced to the students throughout this process. What might seem like a quantifiable target (like "including 22 words in a sentence") is not valid if we would be hard-pressed to find any curriculum document that outlines it as a target for students. What we will find are expectations that focus on voice; sentence fluency; ideas; elements of specific forms of writing; writing with an awareness of audience; using revising, editing, and proofreading strategies effectively; and so on. Each teacher needs to become an expert in his or her own grade's curriculum so that the specific expectations can be woven into the students' learning when it is timely and appropriate to do so. The more familiar a teacher is with the specific curriculum for the grade, the more effective that teacher will be at developing accurate assessment tools with students.

Rubrics Demystified

Rubrics need to be simple and precise tools that are easy to use.

When students understand how rubrics are constructed, they become simple tools through which students and teachers can measure student achievement. In order for students to understand rubrics better, teachers need to develop a clear picture of how to create rubrics themselves. Too frequently, teachers use rubrics that they themselves don't understand. Some rubrics use vague terminology that is difficult to define, and some include measures of things that are not concrete or tangible.

Too often, students are presented with unfamiliar rubrics with certain elements circled or highlighted. I was reviewing one such rubric with a Grade 1 student when he was sharing his writing with me. I asked him to explain what the rubric meant and, of course, he had no understanding of the areas on the rubric, what the levels meant, and even what the term "rubric" meant. The student's teacher, however, certainly felt confident that she was doing the right thing, since she was using a current tool as a way of assessing her students' writing. If the rubric is meaningless to the student, what benefit does the assessment hold? Circling various levels of achievement on a chart has little effect on strengthening student achievement and enabling students to become more reflective writers.

A typical rubric uses a four-point scale ranging from Level 1 to Level 4. With this four point scale in mind, Level 3 is typically the target, where Level 4 exceeds the expectation, and Levels 1 and 2 fall short.

What we should be doing instead is using student-generated success criteria and assisting students in creating their own assessment tools that are meaningful and authentic. Using the success criteria developed at the beginning of the writing process to guide the development of assessment tools enables students to have a thorough understanding of not only the skills that are being assessed, but what they look like in authentic writing samples. When students co-construct the assessment tools, the tools and what they reveal are much more meaningful; students will be able to accurately interpret them and use them for self-reflection, self-assessment, and further goal-setting.

Usually, books for teachers include many ready-to-use teacher- and student-friendly rubrics. This book is different. Although there are rubrics included, they serve only as examples. In the assessment-based writing process, the principal belief is that students need to be integral participants in creating the assessment tools, and this includes the rubrics. That is not to say that the students are setting the standard for their own learning. The teacher remains the one who establishes the expectations, but the students share in the creation of the actual assessment tool: it is created using their words, terms that are meaningful to them and vocabulary that they can easily understand. It is the students' words that define the various levels of achievement.

In this light, students and teachers are able to create their own rubrics, using the success criteria that they have all agreed upon. When the success criteria are used as the Level 3 target on the rubric, it becomes possible to add modifiers to the statements as a way of demonstrating how the work may exceed or fall short of the expectation.

Level 3

Level 3 is the target, the expectation, the skill. This is the level of achievement that we are expecting to see from our students. It needs to be a clear realistic target that is observable and definable. It is a skill that students are able to identify and apply to their work. For example: *My writing expresses a strong emotive voice,* is a measurable, observable expectation. *My writing includes all elements of a* narrative and *My writing includes connections to my prior experiences and background knowledge* are also clear, observable target statements. However, *I have thought about how my reader will connect to this work* is not something that is observable in a written piece of work. *I reflected on the writing process* and *I understand how the elements of a persuasive report fit together* are statements that are difficult to define or measure.

Level 4

Level 4 is the indicator that work has exceeded the expectations. By thoroughly applying the skills, consistently demonstrating their learning, and clearly and creatively integrating new strategies, students are able to go beyond the target that was set. They have, in essence, raised the bar.

Level 2

While Level 4 work exceeds the expectation, work that is Level 2 falls just short. When a student is achieving Level 2, it means that they are able to demonstrate only some of the skill, or are inconsistent in their application of it. They are only nearly-missing the target. They have achieved some of the learning, but may need to continue refining their skills in order to move to Level 3.

Level 1

Level 1 indicates that the student is still at the beginning stages of learning as it pertains to a specific skill. The student is able to demonstrate that skill in limited ways or only with teacher guidance. Students at Level 1 might apply a few of the strategies and require additional support to effectively apply the concept to their work.

Clear Measurable Expectations

Developing clear measurable expectations is a skill that teachers and students can develop together. When the ambiguity of the expectations is removed, it becomes possible for students to identify where their work falls in relation to them. More importantly, they are able to consider what they need to do to move their work to the next level.

Modifiers are the key to writing simple practical rubrics. Once the skill has been defined in clear terms, the statement can be modified to indicate that a piece of work has exceeded or fallen short of the target.

For example, let's take the skill of making connections through writing. If students were able to demonstrate this skill adequately, it would be a Level 3. The statement for the Level 3 might be *My writing includes connections to my prior experiences and background knowledge.*

In order to adjust this statement to reflect Level 4, the modifiers "clearly" and "direct" can be added to the statement. It now indicates that the skill exceeds the expectations: *My writing **clearly** includes **direct** connections to my prior experiences and background knowledge.*

If a piece of work falls just short of the target, the student might still have included some connections. The word "some" could easily change the statement to reflect this shortfall: *My writing includes **some** connections to my prior experiences and background knowledge.*

Finally, Level 1 would indicate that the student made few or no logical connections to prior knowledge through the writing. In the same way, the word "few" changes the statement to reflect this level: *My writing includes few connections to my prior experiences and background knowledge.*

		Sample Rubric: Making Connections		
Skill	**Level 1**	**Level 2**	**Level 3**	**Level 4**
Making connections to prior experiences through writing	My writing includes **few** connections to my prior experiences and background knowledge.	My writing includes **some** connections to my prior experiences and background knowledge.	My writing includes connections to my prior experiences and background knowledge	My writing **clearly** includes **direct** connections to my prior experiences and background knowledge.

As another example, consider the target statement: *My writing includes all elements of a narrative.* In order to truly make this clear for the students, let's define the elements. The Level 3 statement might be *My writing includes all of the elements of a narrative (setting, characters, and a plot with a beginning, conflict, and resolution).*

The Level 4 statement might add the words "creatively" and "effectively."

The Level 2 statement indicates that the writer is almost there; therefore, the statement would include the word "some."

Finally, the Level 1 statement indicates that the writer is at the early stages of developing this skill. The statement can be rephrased into positive-sounding statement.

		Sample Rubric: Narrative Elements		
Skill	**Level 1**	**Level 2**	**Level 3**	**Level 4**
Including the elements of a narrative in writing	I am **beginning** to use a **few** of the elements of a narrative in my writing (setting, characters, and a plot with a beginning, conflict, and resolution).	My writing includes **some** of the elements of a narrative (setting, characters, and a plot with a beginning, conflict, and resolution).	My writing includes all the elements of a narrative (setting, characters, and a plot with a beginning, conflict, and resolution).	My writing **creatively** and **effectively** includes all the elements of a narrative (setting, characters, and a plot with a beginning, conflict, and resolution).

The rubrics on pages 86–88 have been created with sets of success criteria, and are provided as samples. The success criteria have been grouped into skill sets and used as targets for the rubrics. It is important to note that the rubrics provided are intended to serve as guides for teachers and students to construct their personal rubrics.

When you work with students to develop a statement that accurately reflects their targets, it is easy to modify it to represent the different levels of achievement. Think of how meaningful a rubric would be to students if they actually had a hand in creating it rather than having it just presented to them.

Blank templates for creating Success Criteria Feedback Charts (page 89) and rubrics (page 90) with students are provided. By simply using a range of modifiers with the target skill, teachers and students will be able to develop meaningful assessment tools together.

List of Modifiers for Rubrics			
Level 1	Level 2	Level 3	Level 4
Few	*Some*	Identify the target	*Thoroughly*
Little	*Sometimes*		*Clearly*
Irrelevant	*Somewhat*		*Proficiently*
In limited ways	*With some clarity*		*Accurately*
With support	*Occasionally*		*Consistently*
Unclear	*Frequently*		*Skillfully*
Needs more			*Relevant*
I am beginning			*Articulately*
			Concise
			Strong
			Thoughtful
			Effectively
			Complex
			Extensive

Using Exemplars as Measuring Tools

If exemplars are used at the beginning stages of the writing process, they can remain posted throughout the writing process to help guide students thinking, writing, and reflecting.

We use exemplars at the beginning of the writing process as a sample text to establish success criteria; they are also very effective for students to use when reflecting on their learning. Students find it very helpful to keep these sample texts as guides, since they show differing levels of achievement. Young writers are able to reflect on the different levels of writing and determine where their work fits by comparison. Remembering that the assessment-based writing process is reflective and recursive, students are continually encouraged to reflect on the previous stages of writing in order to move forward with their own learning.

Once students are ready to assess their writing, they can compare their work to the work of others and determine which is most similar to their level of achievement. As students measure their writing against the various levels of the exemplars, they will notice the ways in which their writing is similar to other pieces at a similar level. This assists in demystifying the assessment process. Students are not likely to ask "Why did I get a C?" or "How come he got a Level 4 and I got a Level 3?" or "Why did you give me this mark?"

- Students will never again ask why you gave them a specific mark, as they will understand that they earned a certain mark or achieved a given level.

- Students will be able to clearly measure their achievement against a clear standardized set of expectations and exemplars in order to develop an understanding of their current level of achievement.
- Students should be encouraged to share their writing and assessments with each other; rather than asking about the discrepancy in the assessment, they will notice the differences between the pieces of writing and become able to articulate the reasons for the differences in levels of achievement. For example, you might hear, "He got a Level 4 and I got a Level 3 because his ideas are much more developed than mine," or "My writing is a Level 2 because I had some voice in my work. In order to move to a Level 3, I need to make sure that my voice is more apparent in my writing."

When you assess students' work, the most important message you give students is not what level they are currently achieving but what they need to do to move to the next level. As students are active participants in creating the assessment tools, they are soon quick to realize that a Level 2 is not that far from a Level 3, that they are on the right track and are almost there. And then a Level 3 is not that far from a Level 4; they just need to find effective ways of applying and integrating their learning. As students begin to realize how to close the gap between the levels, they will become more reflective in their learning, and begin to articulate their strengths, needs, and next steps. This is the goal of assessment —developing self-regulated self-motivated learners.

Sample Success Criteria: Newspaper Article

Knowledge
- I will demonstrate a good understanding of the parts of a newspaper article.
- I will included the elements of an article (who, what, when, where, why, how).
- I will include the most important ideas at the beginning of my article and the smaller details near the end.

Thinking
- My article will use descriptive writing and will be interesting for the reader.
- My article will include a lot of information that explains the event in a clear manner.

Communication
- I will use correct spelling, grammar, and punctuation.
- My article will be well organized and presented.
- I will use quotes correctly.

Application
- My article will include ideas and evidence to support the main ideas.
- Everything in my article will be important for the reader to know and will be relevant to the story.

Sample Rubric: Newspaper Article

	Level 1	Level 2	Level 3	Level 4
Knowledge	I have included a **few** of the elements of a newspaper article.	I have included **some** of the important elements of a newspaper article.	I have included all of the important elements of a newspaper article.	I have included all of the important elements of a newspaper article, and organized my ideas in **order** of most to least important.
Thinking	My article **needs more** information, or my ideas need to be presented in a clear way. My writing **needs** to be more descriptive and interesting for the reader.	My article includes **some** information, and explains my ideas in a clear way. My writing is **somewhat** descriptive and interesting for the reader.	My article includes enough information, and explains my ideas in a clear way. My writing is descriptive and interesting for the reader.	My article includes **relevant** information, and my ideas are explained in a clear and **concise** way. My writing is descriptive and interesting for the reader.
Communication	My writing has **many errors** in spelling, grammar, punctuation. I **need to** include quotes, or use them more correctly.	My writing has **some** correct spelling, grammar, punctuation. I have used **some** quotes correctly.	My writing has correct spelling, grammar, punctuation. I have used quotes correctly.	My writing has correct spelling, grammar, punctuation. I have used quotes correctly. My writing has **strong** voice, word choice, and sentence fluency.
Application	My article includes **little** evidence to support the main ideas. I have included information that is **not relevant** or important.	My article includes **some** evidence to support the main ideas. The information in the article is **somewhat** relevant and important.	My article includes appropriate evidence to support the main ideas. The information in the article is relevant and important.	My article includes **thoughtful** evidence to support the main ideas. The information in the article is relevant, important and **clearly connected** to the main ideas.

Sample Success Criteria and Feedback: Persuasive Letter

Knowledge
- I will clearly state the problem, my opinion, and the solution (call to action).
- I will use details/evidence to support my opinion.
- I will include an introduction and conclusion that summarize my opinion.
- I will use the form of a letter (salutation, body, closing).

Thinking
- I will use creative language to express a strong emotion.
- My ideas will be logical, reasonable, and organized in a sequence.
- My ideas will be connected to my opinion.
- I will support my ideas with details and reasons.

Communication
- I will use clear expression and logical organization.
- I will clearly present my opinion.
- I will demonstrate formal voice, style, and tone.
- I will use correct conventions (spelling, grammar, punctuation).
- I will demonstrate my word choice (descriptive words, action verbs, appropriate vocabulary).
- My sentences will be fluent and I will use paragraphs.

Application
- My writing will include personal connections to the environment.
- I will use the information from my research to support my opinion.
- I will demonstrate an understanding of how this issue affects others.

Sample Rubric: Persuasive Letter

	Level 1	Level 2	Level 3	Level 4
Knowledge	I have included a **few** of the elements of a letter. My opinion is **not clearly** stated or supported with evidence.	I have included **some** of the elements of a letter. My letter includes an opinion and **some** relevant supporting evidence.	I have included all of the elements of a letter. My letter includes an opinion and relevant supporting evidence.	I have **effectively** and **creatively** included all of the elements of a letter. My letter includes a **strong** opinion and relevant supporting evidence.
Thinking	I have **a few** logical or sequential ideas. My ideas are **not supported** with evidence.	My ideas are **somewhat** creative, logical, and sequential. My ideas are supported with **some** evidence.	My ideas are creative, logical, and sequential. My ideas are supported with detailed evidence.	My ideas are **complex**, creative, logical, and sequential. My ideas are **effectively** supported with detailed evidence.

Sample Rubric: Persuasive Letter continued				
	Level 1	**Level 2**	**Level 3**	**Level 4**
Communication	My writing is **unclear** or shows **limited** organization. I have **not used** appropriate voice, word choice, and sentence fluency. I have **many errors** with conventions (spelling, grammar, punctuation).	My writing is **somewhat** clear and organized. I have used **some** appropriate voice, word choice, and sentence fluency. I have included **some** correct conventions (spelling, grammar, punctuation).	My writing is clear and organized. I have used appropriate voice, word choice, and sentence fluency. I have usually included correct conventions (spelling, grammar, punctuation).	My writing shows a **high degree** of organization and clarity. I have **effectively** used appropriate voice, word choice, and sentence fluency. I have included correct conventions (spelling, grammar, punctuation).
Application	I have used **little** research or personal connections to support my opinion. I **have not** explained how this issue affects others.	I have used **some** research and personal connections to support my opinion. I have explained how this issue affects others in **some** ways.	I have used research and my personal connections to support my opinion. I have explained how this issue affects others.	I have used **extensive** research and my personal connections to support my opinion. I have **thoroughly** explained how this issue affects others.

Success Criteria Checklist and Feedback

Success Criteria *What are the features of an effective piece of writing?*	Self-Reflection
Knowledge: What you write *Including text form, elements, etc.* **Thinking: What you say** *Including ideas, logic, descriptive writing, etc.* **Communication: The way you say it** *Including sentence fluency, voice, conventions, etc.* **Application: The way you connect to it** *Including reasoning, connections, etc.*	Two things I did well: ☺ ☺ Something to think about for my next writing piece: ◯ **Teacher Feedback** *Using the success criteria, provide student with feedback about two things done well, and one suggestion for improvement.*

Rubric

	Level 1	Level 2	Level 3	Level 4
Knowledge				
Thinking				
Communication				
Application				

Student/Teacher Reflections and Goals for Continued Learning:

Conclusion: From Beginning to End... or End to Beginning

The assessment-based writing process is a recursive approach to writing. Using it, students work in collaboration with the teacher to pre-determine the success criteria that will be used to evaluate their work. Students use a range of mentor texts, exemplars, and teacher modeling to set the targets for their own writing. They draft a piece of writing that is consistent with the success criteria. Descriptive feedback is the vehicle through which teachers are able to guide and shape students' writing to closer align with the desired targets. Students are encouraged to revise, rewrite, or retry their writing. The success criteria are able to serve as a constant target for students to work toward. Finally, students are actively involved in turning the success criteria into student-friendly rubrics that effectively evaluate the learning targets.

Now that we have truly reached the End, we are hopeful that you have a good idea of where to begin. Not only is it important that we, as teachers, have a clear understanding of the targets we set for our students; it is equally important that our students have an opportunity to develop a thorough understanding of their learning targets and break them into their individual components. Students need to take an active role in setting the success criteria for their writing and developing the tools that will be used to assess their learning. In summary, only when the end is clear are we ready to begin.

References

Booth, David (2001) *Reading and Writing in the Middle Years.* Markham, ON: Pembroke Publishers.

Brookhart, Susan (2008) "Feedback" *Educational Leadership*, December 2007/January 2008, Association for Supervision and Curriculum Development.

Clarke, Shirley (2003) *Enriching Feedback in the Primary Classroom.* London, UK: Hodder & Stoughton.

Covey, Stephen (1989, 2004) *The 7 Habits of Highly Effective People.* New York, NY: Free Press.

Culham, Ruth (2003) *6+1 Traits of Writing.* New York, NY: Scholastic.

Davies, Anne *What is Assessment For Learning,* www.annedavies.com

Davies, Anne (2008) *Leading the Way to Making Classroom Assessment Work.* Courtenay, BC: Connections Publishing.

Davies, Anne (2008) *Transforming Barriers to Assessment for Learning.* Courtenay, BC: Connections Publishing.

Earle, Lorna M. (2003) *Assessment As Learning, Using Classroom Assessment to Maximize Student Learning.* Thousand Oaks, CA: Corwin Press.

Foster, Graham (2004) *Seven Steps to Successful Writing.* Markham, ON: Pembroke Publishers.

Foster, Graham (2007) *Exemplars: Your Best Resource to Improve Student Writing.* Markham, ON: Pembroke Publishers.

Fullan, Michael (2002) "Principals as Leaders in a Culture of Change" *Educational Leadership.* Special Issue, May 2002. O.I.S.E, University of Toronto.

Gregory, K, Cameron C. & Davies A. (1997) *Setting and Using Criteria.* Courtenay, BC: Building Connections Publishing.

Gregory, K, Cameron C. & Davies A. (2000) *Self-Assessment and Goal Setting.* Courtenay, BC: Building Connections Publishing.

Gunnery, Sylvia (2007) *The Writing Circle.* Markham, ON: Pembroke Publishers.

Hattie, J. & Timperley (2007) "The Power of Feedback" *Review of Educational Research.* American Educational Research Association, Sage Publications.

Jamison Rog, Lori & Kropp, Paul (2004) *The Write Genre.* Markham, ON: Pembroke Publishers.

Lamott, Anne (2005) *Bird by Bird: Some Instructions on Writing and Life.* New York, NY: Random House.

Reid, Janine & Schultze, Betty (2005) *What's Next for this Beginning Writer?* Markham, ON: Pembroke Publishers.

Reid, Steven & Mary (2008) *OWA Ontario Writing Assessment.* Toronto, ON: Nelson.

Routman, Regie (2005) *Writing Essentials.* Portsmouth, NH: Heinemann.

Stiggins, Rick et al (2006) *Classroom Assessment for Student Learning.* NJ: Pearson.

The Ontario Curriculum Grades 1–8, Language (2006) Ontario Ministry of Education.

Trehearne, Miriam (2006) *Comprehensive Literacy Resource for Grades 3–6 Teachers.* Toronto, ON: Nelson.

Acknowledgments

This book came out of the initiatives of a fantastic network of schools. *The Group of 8* is an amazing collection of literacy leaders, who collectively support each other in developing high-yield strategies and best teaching practices. Thanks to the principals and teachers at Walter Scott, Crosby Heights, Ross Doan, Roselawn, Beverley Acres, Michaelle Jean, Charles Howitt, and, of course O.M. MacKillop Public Schools. A special thanks to the chairs of this group, Yvonne West and Bruce Baynham.

Thanks to the professional leadership team of Karen Friedman and Heather Sears, who provided me with invaluable professional development around student-constructed success criteria, descriptive feedback, and assessment for learning. A special thanks to Barb Harold, a fabulous friend, colleague, and partner in literacy. It was great to begin on this journey together, and get *The Write Beginning* off to the right beginning.

How lucky am I? I have had the opportunity to work with some amazing people who have influenced not only my career, but also my life. Thanks to Cheryle Leechman and Yvonne West—two amazing principals in my life: one gave me my roots, and the other my wings. You have forever influenced the teacher I am, and the leader I am learning to be.

Thanks to my amazing literacy partner "back at the ranch," Patty Cassels, who mentored me through my new role seamlessly. You are an amazing friend and partner. Thanks for joining me on this wild ride this year. Also, to the committed, dedicated teaching staff who were so eager to work with me in developing and implementing assessment-based writing strategies. What an honor to work with such a group of professionals, and, of course, the students at MacKillop, who inspire me on a daily basis. A special thanks also to my mentor and very trusted friend Carol Matsoo. I appreciate your constant presence as the "angel on my shoulder" as I navigate the path of life.

How could I write a book about writing without thanking my tireless writing coach and master of descriptive feedback, Kat Mototsune? The strategies that I have brought into my classroom about descriptive feedback I have learned first hand from you. Thanks for making the writing process such an authentic and enjoyable one. Also, a big thanks to Mary Macchiusi for embracing *The Write Beginning* from the start. Every time I write, I am reminded of how fortunate I am to have been given the opportunity to share my work with others. Thanks for your constant encouragement, positivity, and enthusiasm.

A huge, huge, huge thanks again to my amazing family: my children Matthew and Hailey, who graciously gave up playing computer games so that Mommy could have a turn for a while; Mike, who continued to support me with encouragement, food (especially gummy bears), and an understanding tolerance of my far-away, glazed-over look at the dinner table. Finally, thanks to my parents, who are both so supportive of everything I do. Without you…this book may have been only one page long.

Index